THE
NARRATIVE
EDGE

FOREWORD BY EMMY AWARD-WINNING
EXECUTIVE PRODUCER AT THE JIM HENSON COMPANY
HALLE STANFORD

ROD BERGER, PsyD

THE

NARRATIVE

EDGE

AUTHENTIC
STORYTELLING THAT
MEETS THE MOMENT

WILEY

For general information on our other products and services or for technical support, please contact our Customer Care Department within the United States at (800) 762-2974, outside the United States at (317) 572-3993, or fax (317) 572-4002.

Wiley also publishes its books in a variety of electronic formats. Some content that appears in print may not be available in electronic formats. For more information about Wiley products, visit our website at www.wiley.com.

Library of Congress Cataloging-in-Publication Data is Available:

ISBN 9781394331291 (Cloth)
ISBN 9781394331307 (ePub)
ISBN 9781394331314 (ePDF)

Cover Design: Wiley
Author Photo by Jeremy Ryan, www.jeremyryan.art

The Narrative Edge *is dedicated to all the yeses I have received over the years, from interview guests who took a chance on an unproven storyteller to suspicious locals who took a flyer on a traveler searching for a connection.*

In the beginning, anxiety ruled the day. Would cold email outreach yield a yes to an interview? The sweet sound of an email ping flooded my senses each time I read the "yes" to my interview request.

As the years have folded into historical tabs along the path that is my life, I am humbled by the role reversal, which has put me in the position to say "yes" to those hoping I will tell their story. To capture even a sampling of one's story is a privilege I do not take lightly.

I think of myself as the nine-year-old kid with a ball, a pen, and a wish that the ball player would say yes to an autograph. Those who have shared their stories with me have significantly impacted my life, and so today, I dedicate this book to those who believed I had a story and a skill worth capturing.

Contents

Foreword

My life and career are built on stories and storytelling. I've been a television producer at The Jim Henson Company for 30 years, during which my shows have received 23 Emmy nominations (and won for *The Dark Crystal: Age of Resistance* and *Fraggle Rock: Back to the Rock*). I'm now exploring narratives that are dear to me at my own company, Seven Crow Stories. So, I understand stories—and I can recognize kindred spirits who appreciate and love them, too.

Rod is one of those kindred spirits. In his role as a journalist, storyteller, public speaker, and producer, he draws out stories from his interviewees with brilliance, sensitivity, and humor. His own life story is just as astonishing as those of his subjects—who include Pope Francis and Magic Johnson!

I met Rod when he interviewed me for his podcast, *Headroom*, which delves beneath the surface to uncover not only what people do, but also why. I've been interviewed a lot, so it can be difficult not to give canned answers to questions I've been asked a hundred times. But Rod instantly put me at ease. I relaxed and had fun with him, as if I were catching up with an old friend. He didn't ask the same old questions, and as I spoke with him, I found myself thinking about the stories I tell on TV and the stories I tell about myself as if they were fresh and new. It was the best interview I've ever had.

Rod and I kept in touch. It was such a pleasure getting to know him better. What makes him such a good storyteller isn't just that he's curious about people, but he also has an enormous heart. And he's very funny.

I'm currently collaborating with Rod on a series he created with puppeteer Victor Yerrid, with whom I worked on Jim Henson shows like *Sid the Science Kid* and *Dark Crystal: Age of Resistance*. They developed one of the funniest and sweetest ideas I've ever encountered: a show where a goat puppet travels around the world with Rod, interviewing top athletes in search of the ultimate sports GOAT. We haven't sold *Ultimate GOAT* yet, but hopefully someday you'll get to see it.

I was honored when Rod asked me to write the foreword for *The Narrative Edge*. It's a unique book about stories: the stories we share as entertainment, the stories we tell about our careers, and the stories we recount about our own lives. It's a book Rod is exceptionally qualified to write. He comprehends what it means to see yourself as the hero of your own life—and what can occur when you don't. He has learned about storytelling from sources as diverse as refugees from South Sudan, his father, who was a child in WWII Germany, and some of the world's greatest athletes. He distills that knowledge into a book no one else could write.

It's unlike any book on storytelling you've ever read. There are no rules. You don't have to read the chapters in order—in fact, Rod encourages you not to! You don't even need to be a professional storyteller to gain valuable insights from it, as it provides plenty of wisdom about the paths we choose, the career journeys we embark on, and the role of stories in the relationships we cherish. This book on storytelling illustrates its principles by weaving in anecdotes from Rod's fascinating and adventurous life alongside hard-earned wisdom, not only about narratives but about life itself. Rod explores the primal emotions that can either fuel or hinder our stories—shame, love, envy, and honesty—and poses questions that could potentially change our lives.

Where do I find love in my story?

How do cultural influences either suppress or encourage authentic storytelling?

How has conflict shaped who I am today?

How have the different versions of my story served me in various contexts?

What is the narrative arc of my achievements?

These are just a few of the meaningful and enlightening questions that Rod asks. Maybe they will hold the same power for you, or perhaps some of his other questions will. As Rod understands, storytelling is about never settling for easy answers and always pushing yourself to ask the hard questions.

The Narrative Edge doesn't hand you a philosophy of story-telling—it helps you develop your own. Reading it recreates the experience I had when I first met him, when his questions led me to see my stories and life in a new way.

I hope it does the same for you.

—Halle Stanford

Preface

The Narrative Edge sleeps best on your nightstand after a brisk, choose-your-own-adventure, page-turning jaunt through the narrative fields of our lives. Sidle up next to me on a plane to somewhere and share in tarmac tales from distant corners of the earth, revealing the commonalities of being human in a sometimes unforgiving world where stories are the currency of connection.

The role of stories is experiencing a rebirth in our society's collective consciousness. Actively embedded into corporate strategy, educational curricula, and social media platforms, several generations are finding new ways to authentically communicate in an increasingly synthetic world driven by artificial intelligence.

Are we, as a society, ready to keep pace with this storytelling revolution?

Can we edit our stories in real time, or should we dust off the stories imprisoned in the annals of vulnerability and antiquated communication styles to realize the empowering leverage our stories can have on the world around us?

Today's leaders *will* be tomorrow's authors.

The prerequisite to leading a life of intention and impact is our ability to cobble words together, honoring individuality while celebrating community. Our ancestors of storytelling past shone a light on ladders and titles to define a life of accomplishment. Today, leaders from all walks of life are riding a new and expansive horizon line, teetering between linear paths of career prescriptions and rich ecosystems of sustainable workforces and emerging markets.

The need to craft stories that meet the moment *is now*.

The Narrative Edge looks at the benefits of an activated storytelling lifestyle bent on the notion that our stories are personal, strategic, and uniquely us. The question is, "Are you embracing your story at work and home, and if not, why not?"

Together, we'll ride along a candy cane ribbon of stories, twisting people and places into surprisingly familiar and relatable storylines, reminding us that our stories validate our presence and our telling authenticates our experience.

So, will you tell your story or risk having it told by someone or something else?

Introduction

The irony of story is that while we live in an ongoing tale we call our life, we sometimes struggle to acknowledge the filmstrip unfurling right in front of us. We know that story and stories are important—when we pull up a bar stool or chair for a first date, we activate the best face-forward stories we can think of to make a hopefully positive impression.

The beauty of a story, or at least a sliver of its enduring part of our experience, is evidenced in our profound addiction to capturing micro-stories defined by fleeting smiles and moments. For all the skeptics, social media has provided a digital canvas to capture the smell-the-roses moments of our lives. So, at some level, we are all active and passionate storytellers.

I would like to think that I have always been conscious of storytelling. I'd be lying to you and myself, though. I remember being curious about people, places, conversations, and what-if scenarios. I read Choose Your Own Adventure books and dreamt of saving my fellow students from biblical storms, intruders, and catastrophes. For some reason, I routinely ended up as the super-hero saving the day (typed with sarcasm oozing from my fingers).

I distinctly remember summer camp in northern Michigan, staring up at the ceiling of my cabin, dreaming and hoping for more out "there." In sports, I prided myself on having a "motor." If that meant sacrificing my body to save a goal or diving into the stands to start a fast break, I would be first in line. My hunch is that you might have had your version of self-aggrandizing stories that pitted you against the forces of evil or a rival. Not the type of evil Hollywood might brandish across our screens, but rather those experiences and people gracing the filmstrip of our lives.

Ultimately, these initial days of storytelling are private. They are meant to be preserved under the mandate of, do no harm. These audience-of-one stories help us categorize our experiences, ultimately laying a foundation of value propositions many of us hold onto through adulthood.

As we age, we discover that our stories frequently intersect with our careers, social declarations, and personal experiences.

It was the winter of 2023, that point north of New Year's Day just shy of Valentine's Day, and I was again staring up at the stars—this time in Eastern Africa—holing up in a refugee camp on a mission to learn about storytelling among Africans over several generations and dark chapters of colonization from multiple European countries. As part of an NGO contingent, I aimed to learn about the characters and traditions that maintained personal and cultural dignity in the face of relentless attacks.

I spent my days canvassing small sectors of homemade brick homes the size of posh closets back home, looking to understand better the story's value to the collective voice spread across approximately 70,000 refugees, many of whom fled persecution in South Sudan.

This was a point of heightened attention for me, as I was simultaneously composing my first TEDx Talk, which would be given in just a couple of weeks in sunny and affluent

Tampa, Florida. To be clear, I had been incredibly fortunate to be trusted with the stories of celebrities, professional athletes, heads of state, royals, and transcending minds worldwide.

Those were one-of-one experiences captured for audiences through articles, podcasts, and photography. But now I had to get into the kitchen of storytelling, evaluate the gumbo of stories I had already captured throughout my career, and eventually find a through line.

A theme.

A notion of influence through the sometimes pungent experiences of others reflecting on journeys, not of glory but of sacrifice. At that moment, after a long, hot, and dry day, I closed the door to my hut to compose my Talk, and I realized a fundamental but consequential truth about my own life. If I were to draft a powerful message about a story, I first had to expose the bruising of my character within the very stories I had been assigned to capture.

This teensy kernel is a buried treasure for those curious enough to pick up this book. As we all go into the cold, dark night of the future, our ability to feel the stories of others within the fabric of our historical tapestry will help us author powerful and impactful futures of value.

The Narrative Edge acknowledges the power of stories in our effort to affix value to our experiences, opinions, grievances, passions, pursuits, and those days that start sunny and close under cover of gloom. Stories and those that define each of us continuously chronicle our lives, moment by moment, in the shadows or under the bright lights of attention. As your guide, I am responsible for identifying the power of the moments we shirk responsibility from, celebrate, or bristle at.

The world we know is changing at light speed, and if we are to bend the horizon through our positive contributions and influence on others, then we must attack life in the spirit of a novelist, not merely a witness.

I'll never quarrel over storytelling rules. I'll never ascribe one method over another.

I will, though, request that you treat this book like you do in the relationships that mean the most to you. Take me, if you will, as you tear out of your home, racing to school or work. Close your eyes and thumb through the pages as though you're randomly choosing one apple over another in the produce section. *The Narrative Edge* isn't meant to be a linear experience. Read Chapter 4 first if you like. Cobble together a Saturday afternoon with Chapters 7, 9, and 2, or reread this introduction on the tarmac while waiting for your flight to take off.

These are your stories. Not mine. My experiences are meant to crack open the door to the power you hold in the messiness of life. Meeting the moments before us requires a willingness to ask the tough questions, not of others necessarily, but of ourselves. If I sat down to have coffee with you, how willing would you be to answer these questions:

- How do the stories we tell ourselves shape our understanding of who we are?
- Why do we sometimes struggle to acknowledge the stories unfolding in our own lives?
- What's the difference between recording moments and truly capturing stories?
- How might becoming more conscious of your personal narratives transform your relationships?

The notion of willingness might sound laden with a prerequisite age to fully appreciate the tenets of this book. Contrary to popular or unpopular positions, I have always been an advocate of stories from those of all ages, backgrounds, perspectives, and opinions—meaning, this book has been constructed for students of life including actual students in high school or university, parents, entrepreneurs, CEOs who've been told they need to be a better storyteller to influence the masses, artists compelled by one art form and inspired by narrative interpretation of life, to the single parent dreaming of future opportunities or teams and communities of shared beliefs aspiring to meet the moment … to appreciate the pursuit and rewrite tired and unrepresented narratives.

The seeds of the story should be cultivated across our lifespan. Delicate, sure. Meant to be tumbled through life on high heat, yes. Wrinkle-free stories are facades masquerading as life. The value we ascribe to our stories is just that—in our control at every juncture, regardless of the punctuation of life's ups and downs.

As you stride, stroll, or run through the book, note that each chapter begins and ends with an original six-word story paying homage to the celebrated story or myth of Ernest Hemingway's brief but powerful storytelling. Legend has it that he was challenged by other writers, and in response, he quipped that he could write a compelling story in a mere six words. *The Narrative Edge* borrows the powerful technique to level-set given chapters and the questions utilized to boil down our stories into elements of authentic representation. We will bob and weave across the world's continents, picking up stories steeped in emotion, relative to our lives, and those a galaxy away.

I invite you into my life of rewrites, exclamation points, pregnant pauses, and commas, which reflect the curiosities of life, not the answers.

1 | Origin Stories

The Relationship We Have with the Story of Us

Story for sale. Barter or cash.

It could have very well been the late 1970s, but I'm leaning toward the early 80s when I experienced what was as real as I could have ever imagined at that age—a sighting of the real Santa Claus! It was Christmas Eve, and my plan was about to unfold—one eye open and my ears alert. You see, I had set up a walkie-talkie near the television in our living room, hoping against all hope I'd catch a whistle or a "ho, ho, ho" crackling over the radio waves into my bedroom—the first door at the top of the stairs.

Tossing and turning, I didn't trust my walkie or its ability to "talkie," so I scanned the upstairs—first with my ears, then with my eyes as I crept out of bed. I was in the clear and thankful for the proximity of my room to the stairs. Ever so quietly, I sleuthed my way down the stairs, hyper-vigilant not to get caught.

I felt both excited and terrified! As a kid, any strange man dressed in a red suit was bound to scare the living daylights out of me. When I placed my right palm on the final banister, I heard a noise. I couldn't tell if it was coming from behind me, beside me, or in front of me!

I took a chance and rushed straight to the kitchen.

Nothing!
The sounds stopped.

I peered into the living room and saw the corner of a box that might be a present—okay, I knew I wasn't going crazy. I settled under a couch-back table just deep enough for my scrawny body to hide. I heard the carpet sink repeatedly, as if it was being squished by something. I took a risk—I nudged my head above the glass-top table, narrowly missing the clothes-snagging propertics of the cheapest wicker, and looked toward the TV.

There he was! I couldn't see his face, but I knew it was him! I saw the red, darker than I had imagined, but the white trim and boots—oh, yeah, that was him.

★ ★ ★

I never spoke to Santa that night. In fact, I don't remember anything after that brief glimpse. I woke up on Christmas morning in my bed, wondering if what felt so real was simply my imagination. All these years later, our family tradition is to watch *The Polar Express* (2004) before I read *'Twas the Night Before Christmas* to the kids. That movie gets to me every time. Like the young boy in the film, I still hear the bell ringing on Christmas Eve, and I am convinced it echoes back to my own adventure that night in the suburbs of Detroit.

Throughout the years, I have had opportunities to reflect on the stories buried deep within me through the percussion of life's accomplishments from those I've been privileged to interview. In truth, I've always loved the feeling I get when the questions in my mind are answered through the melody of a story.

Only as an adult have I come to recognize that sometimes stories fill in the gaps of our fractured experiences and relationships, forging new, acceptable narratives that we can live with. I'm not sure why the memory of Santa remains so clear to me today, but I trust that experience served a purpose, both then and now.

Forged from hate. Released in death.

The second hand marched over my wrist. Each second clamped down like the boots of the SS over wet cobblestone. "It can't be this loud." The voice of frothing disgust echoed throughout my head. Was the quiet in the boarding hall too quiet? I asked myself.

Tonight was the night I shouted across the walls of my skull. Not a peep seeped out by the grace of God. Sweat from my smooth, childish brow couldn't hold on, leaking down the bridge of my nose to the tip of my chin.

Mummified with fear, I struggled to control my unraveling mind.

Slowly counting, I found a sense of peace blanketing my mind. If only the covers were as forgiving in this coffin-like slab I lay on. There was no time to file away complaints nor a receptive audience.

A long breath from my toes down the runway of my silhouette, Zehn, neun, acht, sieben, sechs, fünf, vier, drei, zwei, eins ...

Ever so slowly, my teeth decisively bore into my cheek. Clenching somehow convinced me that I was even stealthier peeling the sandpaper sheets from my scrawny, concave shoulders below my waist. A feeling of cool air filled my torso, and a wave of adrenaline billowed to my fingertips.

Deadly shadow puppets began to file past an interior window like clockwork.

I had 17 minutes before the retread of rubber clogged methodically through the halls.

My legs twisted over my stomach before dropping my toes one by one onto the hollowed-out grooves of the plank floor. Noise was my enemy as I raised my wrist within an inch of my nose.

Fifteen minutes … tick, tick, tick …

Shallow breaths kept my pace—no time to dawdle.

On my knees, like a good Catholic, I lurched my right arm under my bed, about a click behind my footlocker. My fingers latched onto the oblong box.

Twelve-and-a-half minutes to my stretched eye, I was peering back as I secured the catch.

Tonight, I take control. I get the answers to the questions bleeding through my body as I brought the shortwave radio to my chest not unlike a mother desperately clinging to her baby in a bombed-out shelter.

I slunk across the floor—the supply closet in my sight.

I could feel the seconds tapping me, telling me to hurry up.

Maybe ten minutes. The absoluteness of the closet refused even a morsel of ambient light to hit my watch face.

Extending my arm, the third shelf from the bottom, a tattered pillow lay with the smell of rotted potatoes emanating across its cotton fibers. But, for me, a glorious silencer. Smashing the pillow over my nose, I inhaled the stench of thankfulness.

Huddled against the back wall, I turned the dial from left to right.

Click, click, ting, ting, English voices began whispering into my numb ear. Squeezing the mouth of the Englishman against me, undoubtedly leaving an imprint of iron mesh waffles, was worth its weight in day-old bread.

Thank God I spoke English. Each noun was followed by a devastating adjective, piercing everything I thought I knew.

I scrambled to secure my watch face flush with my left ear—tick, tick, tick.

Maybe three minutes. I had heard enough.

Ever so quickly, I disengaged my now-aching ear and turned the dial counterclockwise, invoking a single shutdown click.

Slithering across the uneven floor, I somehow slotted the radio into its safe zone and, like a spider, meticulously made my way back into the living coffin of compliance.

Short bursts of heels rooting told me night duty was circling back. Every bodily system had thankfully gone dormant to shutter any late-night inquiries laced with cold metal whiplashes.

My eyes!

My eyes!

I couldn't close the hatches. Desperate to lunge out of my head, I knew I had to batten down the only remaining proof of insubordination.

Rhythmic rubber notes crescendoed at the edge of my hairline, passing the horizon of one lonely flickering overhead hallway light.

I was in the clear.

My youthful body forever changed. A cold chill of reality made its way up and under my covers.

I was them. They are killers.

What. Am. I?

★ ★ ★

It's 1988, and that courageous boy born of hate, my father, was driving me to sleepaway camp deep in the wooded Michigan landscape. My father was a man of few words; a man with endless disappointing stares and canyon-deep dark eyes.

The curiosity of a young German boy snatched by the Nazis had long migrated to a storage facility, in wait, for the next reincarnated go-round. I just had no idea today would be that day. Let's talk a bit about who my father was in the chapter of his life that included me.

He silently embodied a communication style that was sterile and static, void of hopes and dreams. I knew this even when he bellowed short, staccato explosions filled with past grievances, giving a skewed runway of rationale to whatever currently irked him.

We didn't exchange stories. If I'm honest, we participated in status reporting. Stories about school or girls or anything that resembled a Fred Savage monologue in an episode of the 1980s hit *Wonder Years* be damned.

Maybe I had a bit of his courage in me, or perhaps it was the oppressive silence as we meandered through the *mitten* of Michigan. Perhaps I was curious. Either way, this was my opportunity to ask the questions I had swirling around.

"Dad, can we talk about the war?"

My father arched his rigid frame against the 90-degree angle of his cloth driver-side seat, glanced at me, and asked, "Are you sure you want to know?"

My inner voice quickly responded, clearly out of sync with my actual voice—time froze. I calmly collected my thoughts and answered yes—not too eagerly, as that could easily scare my father's stories back into his secret vault.

It worked.

His receptiveness puzzled my tween brain, but I wouldn't show my amazement. Harrowing stories flowed out like oak barrels cascading over Niagara Falls.

I couldn't keep up.

I began to feel pride, puzzlement, and a desperate need for clarity. I had said *yes*, and I might as well have swallowed the red pill like Neo in the cult classic *The Matrix*. Reflecting on my father's memories answered the question that had held me back for years: What happened to this man I revere?

Years later, I found myself on the stoop of a tenement dwelling on the outskirts of Hollywood glamour. Maybe that's a bit overboard, but it felt less like a home and more like a residential bus stop compared to the wealth surrounding me.

It was a pivotal point in my life.

I felt lost at sea, surrounded by a desert of wannabes, trying to determine what life had in store and whether I had the strength to fully embrace it without second-guessing. I had a jumble of dirty laundry words, phrases, anecdotes, and moments all mixed together. No story.

I wasn't sitting next to my father, but I remember feeling as if I were him. The Hollywood night teetered between today and tomorrow, and I had to make a decision. I had been accepted into a doctoral program in clinical psychology. An investment of time and money was at stake. As I sat there with an old and much wiser friend, I waded into the murky waters of doubt.

This friend asked me a fundamental question—"Do you plan on being alive in seven years?"

Hmm …

I quickly felt my head sink into my shoulders, almost like bracing myself before surgery. I was back in the van, heading up to summer camp with my dad. I had agreed to his vault of soul-stealing stories and was captivated by the power of choice—or the lack of it. We rolled our minivan through the log-borne camp gates, and I distinctly remember my dad marking the moment—his message was for me to pursue as many degrees as I could and embrace educational opportunities, since that would probably be the only tool I'd have to navigate a world full of unknowns.

The essence of our father-son moment poignantly delivered to me that day wasn't about avoiding violence or hate. It was about the answer, the response to life, about getting ahead of the clouds while the masses looked on in amazement at the swirling, tumultuous winds above.

It was about owning a story—*my story*.

★ ★ ★

Sometimes, it makes sense to start at the end. However, conclusions risk combining outcomes with fears. As you and I embark from the dock of life, we must address a few tricky issues that will arise as we move through the book.

First, we must release the control that most of us desire. Our connection to stories and their resulting value comes from others, not ourselves. Sure, we stumble about as toddlers, creating stories with every adorable thing we do, even though we will most likely never recall them.

Stories shape who we are and what our names mean and represent. Some of us are juniors, while others represent firsts or seconds. Some may have once been unwanted but are now treasured. The starting blocks of life, though shared over hours and days, are unique to each individual. As much as we may want to escape those initial stories, they live rent-free in our minds, our forgotten yet never lost dreams and nightmares. It's a blend of time and space where control is not part of our calculus, but rather in the hands of those entrusted with our care.

★ ★ ★

The end can signify a rebirth or, at the very least, an opportunity to create a new chapter. Let's take a walk together. Let's journey back to the barren landscape of Eastern Africa, as I briefly mentioned in the introduction to this book.

I have mostly lived in relative, if not tenuous, control of the story where I am the main character. Despite lacking money at various points in my narrative, I have still been able to make significant decisions, enabling me to rise to the occasion. There is something truly empowering about making choices, yet many people are born into conflict or strife, in unfamiliar lands and makeshift beds, where the opportunity to take control of their lives is like a flame without flint.

The drive from Kampala, Uganda, to the Imvepi Refugee Settlement was supposed to take roughly six to seven hours across nauseous paths. Tack on another five hours for this Mzungu, a Bantu word meaning wanderer or white person. The slow churn of the front axle brought the eyes of darkness upon us as the remaining minutes of the day bid all of us a good night. The dark, weathered, and worn skin of the refugees bled into the darkness along the roadway, only the whites of their eyes could reveal.

There would be no hiding for me. My newfound characters and I would share the story of assumption. I couldn't escape my skin or the fear that had been imposed upon me by Westerners of all kinds. I was entering a land within a land where my truths were myths and my perceptions were biased. As we slowly rolled into camp that night, I had never been more aware of my presence.

Have you ever found yourself in a movie theater, almost watching yourself as you become engrossed in the mythical tale unfolding before you? When the characters' emotions resonate deeply with your desires or struggles at that moment, it can lead you to reflect, "*I want that*" or "*I've been there before.*"

As I was led to my hut, I knew this was a film, unfolding in real time, just for me. I wanted to absorb every emotion, capture every fleeting glance, and witness each new vista as a love letter to a culture and human experience I had never known.

I was there to understand the role that stories played across generations affected by colonization at the hands of European conflict, though often reported as the result of fair negotiation. The stories consistently featured a hare character facing the beasts of the day, seeking safety and stability through the value of representative narratives. One afternoon, as I wandered through a landscape reminiscent of scorched earth scenes from apocalyptic films with residents burning the land in preparation for the rainy season, I came across a story that needed to be told.

Remember when I said we would first crack open the ending to understand the beginning?

Mawa Emmanuel

A man circling the sun for the 25th time sat just outside a group of women storytelling through song and dance. The day had begun to shift into the early evening hours, and dusk was just moments away from revealing itself. A man with an unusual name gazed in my direction. I felt as though I was being given an invitation.

I casually and respectfully approached him. His age was hard to determine. A resigned expression, hardened by tragedy, was the only conclusion I could reach.

Dark. Sad. Eyes.

I remember feeling worried, not for my safety, but for respecting what he wanted to share or not share with a stranger and his surroundings. A slow and methodical discussion started. Scratch that. It was more of an exchange of a few words at a time, as if we knew each other was there, yet hidden amid the rubble of history and disenfranchisement. I've been fortunate enough to interview more than 4,000 people worldwide, yet the most impactful moment, though informal by necessity, was this conversation with Mawa Emmanuel.

I felt out of control. I wasn't even certain where the thread of the story began or ended, and I desperately craved more. Over the course of three additional encounters, I learned that Mawa is a label or descriptor—an approach to the naming convention used in various parts of the world to signify the context of one's birth. Emmanuel was born during wartime, and Mawa pinpointed his time of birth as the time-stamping rings of evidence surrounding the fibers of the earth's trees.

A point in time to remember.

A moment in time to honor the impact of loss.

A *scarlet letter* for Mawa Emmanuel.

In no way is this an attempt to be trite, but what if Vietnam preceded either your or my first name? This historical tattoo impacted Emmanuel, deepening his narrative that his life was unrealized. At 25, his only living family member, his mother, had decided to leave him alone at the refugee camp. Her story lingered in limbo, leaving her wanting, wondering, and wavering between the harsh realities of refugee life and the fog of war. She needed to know who was gone, so she traveled back to South Sudan, leaving behind the comforts of an outdoor prison-like existence for a higher calling.

Emmanuel, too old to remain in the settlement's school, spent most days where I found him—lost in his thoughts, sitting in a random plastic outdoor chair you might see tipped over outside a rural gas station in the United States.

I distinctly remember when my curiosity collided with my emotionally driven need to find a silver lining in Emmanuel's story. I asked him about hope, wrapping it in future aspirations—not out of sheer ignorance, I hope, but in a way that suggested we were sharing a moment. I may not have known the origin of Emmanuel's story beyond his displacement from South Sudan as a teenager to Imvepi. Still, I will never forget the experience of reaching a shared conclusion that contrasted sharply with my beliefs about life. Emmanuel stoically expressed his deep desire to become a doctor while also conveying the purgatory of a dead-end road.

No money.

No medical school.

No next page, much less a chapter, before a third decade of traveling around the sun.

I had never experienced an ending before *the* end. Despite the instinct deep inside me to course-correct the dead-end narrative I was presented with, I couldn't. I tried with everything I had—an extremely biased desire to give him sunlight in an otherwise dark and terrible tale of truth.

The lessons learned that day continue to haunt me. The questions I never had the chance to ask inflict a reckoning that the realities of my life are merely a short story in the tattered fabric of the global human experience.

I have known this in my head, but I hadn't welcomed this truth into my heart.

* * *

As we create this book together, we need to have a heart-to-heart conversation within the syllabic dance found among its pages. We can visit a refugee camp together. We can transport ourselves back to times defined more by facial hair trends, the color palettes of cars and furniture, and smoking sections. Yet, we still arrive at the same conclusion: questions give rise to answers, and without questions, we are left lifeless.

The trick or treat of storytelling lies in using questions to outline the field of play. Once we establish a solid foundation with the stories that represent us, we gain more than just a fighter's chance to participate in editing our lives.

Some might say, "Easier said than done."

Why? Well, many of us live in a perfection-seeking society. Can we express our experiences through the simple act of asking questions that might suggest we were wrong or misguided in our previous beliefs? *Homo sapiens* (meaning "thinking man") highlights our unique ability to think and reason, distinct from our ancestral primate relatives. Part of that tremendous responsibility involves being able to differentiate intention from experience to free ourselves from guilt; otherwise, we risk living defensively rather than actively engaging with all the narratives available to us. And if we wish for a world that embraces the richness of our personal and professional stories, we must reduce the volume of external noise.

We'll never truly grasp the real market value of our stories or the currency they hold in our communities, countries, or families without activating a simple premise to get us started:

It's not your fault.

It's not your fault.

It's not your fault.

Robin Williams's passionate, direct declaration to Will Hunting, portrayed by Matt Damon in the coming-of-age classic *Good Will Hunting* from the early 2000s, effectively *illustrates* the concept of what I term *assignment*: the idea that for our stories to flow down the narrative river, we inherently assign values, judgments, biases, classifications, and representations to all living things and the contexts in which they are presented to us.

For those of you who share my experience of parenthood, you witness this unfold daily. One child starts a tale of justification with an *accusation* about how terrible their sibling is. Friends and coworkers start their solo rebellion, amplifying traits attributed to the perceived villain as the ultimate obstacle to their efforts. We will never remove this emotional piston, meant to protect us, from firing within our internal engines.

Will Hunting tells a semi-classical American story about a young person who feels unloved and has a hidden talent waiting to be recognized by others. As the emotionally troubled character starts to reconcile his past with his present choices, he keeps a stoic demeanor: "I've got this." I won't speak for you, but I can share moments when I put on a strong exterior to conceal the deeper narrative beneath the surface.

Once we clear away self-doubt, we can pose questions that will uncover the true value of the currency we wish to trade with the world around us. So, join me in taking a deep breath as we slowly and methodically place one foot in front of the other. The benefit of our relationship is that I won't hear the answers to the following questions whispered, bellowed, or scoffed at.

I'm treating the following questions as a mix-and-match exercise, allowing you to choose your own adventure. There is no recommended order or correct answer. The questions are designed to help us establish a better and more solid foundation in the stories that define us, uplift us, and empower us in personal and professional journeys we are proud to embrace.

Let's go! I'll provide context for each question, but please understand that your life and interpretation could vary wildly, which is okay.

How Much of Your Story Has Been Authored at the Hands of Others?

Control. Do you have it? Have you ever had it? I reflect on my days working in mental health settings, conducting intake assessments—the initial meeting with a client to better understand the history of their current challenges. I vividly remember clients and patients of all ages and backgrounds expressing a sense of detachment from the circumstances that negatively influenced the trajectory of their lives.

The brass tacks about our origins are that they are what they are—histories, while needing a rewrite, are set in stone. The lessons, however, are malleable if we're willing to chip away at the edges to better understand our relationship with the concept of control.

Have You Ever Been the Main Character in Your Origin Story?

If the answer to this question is no, why not? Did you have a sibling who joined you in the family? Were there life-altering circumstances that pushed your character to the background? Perhaps a parent served in the military, or one parent left the nuclear family due to divorce or passed away? Several storylines have the potential to reshape our narratives.

I remember a woman who told me that she never had a bedroom while growing up. She was confined to the family room, not because there wasn't enough space in the house for her to have a room of her own. From the beginning, she was not seen as having a leading or primary role. Throughout her life, she pursued the bright lights of newfound love, exotic relationships, and children who were celebrated for their public achievements.

Have You Ever Been Asked What Character You Want to Be or Play?

We are initially assigned roles within the family unit, which then transform into neat little cubicles in classrooms. Then we blink and become "that" person in a fraternity or sorority, the break room, the site, the boardroom, the stage, and as a partner, parent, or spouse.

What Story Best Describes Your Entrance onto the Stage?

My late father would likely have shared a World War II story to describe his entrance into this world. If I had to guess, it might be one where he was chased by American GIs trying to steal his wristwatch. As a boy under seven in the story, his recounting was often marked by a wry smile because he could outlast or outrun the GIs, maintaining his ability to tell time while keeping some semblance of dignity.

Mawa Emmanuel. This may sound somewhat cliché, but if I have any regret in life, it's that I never had that "next" conversation with him. The pain from his intense gaze as he sat in his wobbly plastic chair haunts me, especially in light of this question. I genuinely believe he might be more inclined to lead with his exit rather than his entrance. Understandably, he exudes a sense of being hollowed out by war, where the stage he thought he would enter had already been destroyed. The lesson of contemplating the ending or exit shouldn't be overlooked—we risk becoming prisoners of the moment. The state of our jobs, relationships, success, or lack thereof can restrict our ability to think genuinely about our why.

A benefit of reflecting on our entrances and exits is understanding the steps needed to navigate each path. Can we identify the story elements, whether historical or forward-looking, that influence our story's success or failure in personal and professional markets?

Don't answer any of the questions above this line.

You read that correctly. Let's give each other a break.

Storytelling can be challenging, but that's okay. Let's start with an area of adult life that provides shade to the bright and intense light of our personal life.

★ ★ ★

Our professional lives and the origin of our overarching story are likely reflected in our LinkedIn profiles and resumes. As before, let's explore questions that, when edited, embody our professional lives rather than our personal ones.

What might we learn about the value of our story?

Quite frankly, we have all been conditioned to view our professional lives as a BLT (bacon, lettuce, and tomato) sandwich—each ingredient, experience, role, or position represents something above or below an achievement. Mixing and matching story elements (ingredients) sequenced just right, like a leaf of lettuce balancing atop the gluttonous ridges of bacon, hopefully provides a mouth-watering tale of what it would be like to work with you.

The only parallel in our personal lives would center around life-altering events—birth, death, divorce, moves, marriages, and graduations. I don't know about you, but I can't imagine a list of such shining or regretful milestones being on full display beyond mosaic photo blasts memorializing events on Facebook.

How does our perception shift if we rephrase the original question? (How much of your story is authored by others?)

How Much of Your Resume Is by Design or Accident?

It would be incredibly satisfying, at least for me, to declare that my professional story was mapped out from the beginning. This would grant me some equivalent of magical powers, suggesting that I held the pen to the achievements that define me as a person—sharing or telling our resumes presents a narrative opportunity to add meaning to our choices.

The challenge is that if we share a story devoid of life's messy traits, we detach ourselves from authentic engagement with those who could represent our colleagues, leaders, and visionaries. The adage that we hire those we want to work with resonates strongly against a backdrop of choreographed narratives focused on outcomes rather than journeys. One reason we struggle in this area of story sharing is the role we have played or, rather, the significance of our participation in the outcome. When we interview for a job or any professional opportunity, we face the dilemma of conveying the roles we've held alongside the successes we highlight.

Too much?

Too little?

Under the umbrella of professional opportunity, these exchanges create distinctive chances to express the impact you've made and aspire to make in the future. Let's revisit the question—Have you ever been the main character in your origin story?—and apply the key elements to professional experiences. We find ourselves examining the significance of professional chapters in relation to personal story outcomes.

If we don't like the answer, many turn to entrepreneurship—the professional equivalent of securing a publishing deal and controlling the narrative and vision for a new story.

Regardless of how you or I feel about our own origin stories—whether we need to adopt an agree-to-disagree approach with others who have co-written or co-opted our narratives—it is crucial that we give ourselves time to celebrate both the small and significant moments, confront challenges with respect for ourselves and our experiences, and actively revise as the only playwright responsible for the storylines of our future.

To meet the moment of our lives and issue stories that influence and impact those around us, we must come to our own Armistice Day (Veteran's Day before being changed in 1954 under President Dwight D. Eisenhower). This is a day on which we lay down *assignments* for ourselves and others in an act of self-care.

The stories that define us and those we hold in high regard serve as life-explaining markers in the winding journey of being human in the 21st century. Past stories blend into our current narratives, creating a cycle of human emotions that will shape the paths of tomorrow. You don't need to read the palm of humanity to assert the ongoing effort to address the big question of why we are here. We will continue to ponder our origin story, consistently favoring elements that uplift while dismissing narratives that undermine our hopes and dreams.

I recently interviewed an internationally renowned historian, author, and university professor specializing in Nazi Germany and National Socialism. After completing the interview, I delved into personal memories to share stories from that winding road up the mitten of Michigan decades ago. In particular, I recounted the story described in the opening scene of this chapter about a boy, part of the infamous Hitler Youth, risking life and limb to uncover the truths behind those spreading hate across his country and the world.

My guest did not challenge the principles of Hitler Youth. There were certain fundamental criteria that the Nazis adhered to in their recruitment process, aimed at solidifying future leadership should the Third Reich achieve global dominance. I knew my account was not a fabrication and that, at the very least, the foundational elements were based on solid historical evidence. But I could feel the threads of my narrative being gently pulled by this accommodating and thoughtful expert. With a nod to my receptiveness, he adjusted his eyeglasses. He suggested an inaccurate version, blending fact and fiction for a more plausible narrative than the Hollywood rendition I had been given.

If I accepted his request to investigate the merits of my father's story, I would risk losing a memory that has been, for as long as I can recall, a source of pride in my effort to understand the tale of a broken man and a boy who just wanted his dad. As a father, I chose to embrace the professor's digital hand and open myself to a gentle form of scrutiny.

In short, recounting the story I remember would be challenging to reconcile, the man shared. I realized this the moment I sensed doubt from the professor. I politely thanked him for his graciousness—I believe he understood the significance of the story to me, but the historian in him couldn't resist the enticing fact staring him right in the face. He proceeded to take me through historical realities that revealed the fantastical elements of the story I had cherished for so long. I hope I can approach this human moment with the same class and respect he showed.

Since that interview, I have internally battled between my hope for my father's story and cynically reflecting on all the tales shared about that fateful day riding up to summer camp.

Maybe my father wanted to be the superhero in the stories he shared, not out of vanity, but to preserve the role he hoped to play, though circumstances ultimately took the lead. Regardless, I now have an alternative storyline along the fatherly branch of my family tree to ponder.

The origins of our lives are likely filled with entanglement, disappointment, and fear, along with pleasantries and nostalgia— all of which are valuable for deconstructing the role that story plays in the currency we exchange with the world. Our choices can be summed up in the following question:

Do Our Origin Stories Build Us Up Authentically or Shake Us Down in Reality?

If you're like me, the answer varies between what I hope for and what I know to be true. There are stories that instill pride for the moments we desperately need affirmation and those that fill the scenes of our lives with context, even if the reality depicts a life of have-nots.

Mawa Emmanuel and my father embody the power of story, whose origins can be disclosed chronologically or retrospectively, authentically, and in reality. The value of our story and the currency of how we tell it offer a fluid opportunity to understand ourselves and the reasons behind our motivations and fears.

Before you finalize this page, I encourage you to revisit the questions about your origin story—not the professional inquiries, but those that may connect to more profound and impactful narratives. The journey ahead will bring both of us closer to recognizing the authentic moments that uniquely provide an edge to the narratives we live by.

Return to sender. New home address.

2 | Love Stories

Falling in Love Again with the Stories That Define Us

It won't sting. It will hurt.

Dear Me,

It isn't often that I sit down and pen my thoughts about you. I can't shake you, and even when I want to, I feel the tug of your words, "… trust the universe." I don't want to wash away this feeling. There has to be a lesson hidden in all of the pain. Every step forward lurches me back to insecurity. I am unsure what you or I could have done differently, and I don't want to ever lose the dreamer in either of us.

I'm angry. I'm f$#@&* angry! I am tired of always looking over my shoulder, wondering, outright panicking at the sound of the mail truck or the ring of the front door … to be served! What did I do? What did I do???

Five years born out of necessity, down the drain, and all I have left is a story.

A costly story.

"So, this aw-shucks guy meets a famous entrepreneur, goes into business with him, soaks up the lathered compliments in sheet cake stretches only to find out he was aboard a trojan horse."

Wait. Wait. I have a better opening line to my own Lifetime Sad Sap movie.

"Unassuming dolt unwittingly gets tagged with company debt while lying in a hospital bed with COVID-19, hoping to save the company and employee hearts from financial ruin."

Now that's good. A pandemic. A hospital bed. I might as well sound like a wounded soldier reflecting on the battlefield under the canvas tents of presumed safety. I will give you this—you went into the venture with both feet and gave everything you had, but in the end, you were burned by the very thing that got you as far as you did—your devotion and maybe a dose of drunk dreamer syndrome.

Your story was romantic. It was about building something from nothing. Seeing an opening that others had glided by.

And. You. Failed.

It's okay. We all fail; if we don't, we haven't lived. I am writing this letter to you and me because I need and want to grieve the loss of the company, the temporary loss of dignity, and the dream that was most likely manufactured out of necessity, not gut. Losing a job and starting a company without pausing has its limits on our psyche. I know that now, and I needed to know it then.

That's why we had so many dark moments we couldn't share with anybody. Our best friends. Our wife. Our family. Nobody.

Time does heal, and time grants perspective to those willing to buy a ticket to the matinee where we are the withering star. If I'm honest with you, the most challenging moments were when the supposed movie played out on cold nights, battling the steering wheel of fate.

I've realized that the yellow line dividing us from oncoming traffic is as much about prevention as reality. There were many lonely moments when crossing that line seemed easier and cleaner than putting my family through lawsuit hell without a shovel. Meandering in and out of yellow lines reminded me of the maybe or maybe not true story that my grandfather accidentally killed someone while he drove his Greyhound bus decades ago. I'm just glad I could find you each time my tires veered and my knuckles rolled.

It's funny how random storylines creep up when we least expect it. I don't know much, but my love meter for you is finally leaning in the right direction. I've been absent but not gone. I've been quiet, not silent.

I've been patient.

Losing a company at the hands of evil runs the risk of painting one a professional lepper. I haven't, and I won't let that happen to you and me ever again. I've loved our story. Some chapters are painful to read, but if I do say so myself, the character ... our character ... is fascinating.

So, as we close the chapter on a page-turner that has been five years in the making, let's remember that the story can change, but the character remains.

You are good. I am good.

We are good.

Cherry Picking

Shame—a powerfully descriptive, guttural word that implies some level of wrongdoing and can take hold of the steering wheel of our lives right under our noses. Each of us experiences the story of shame differently, often shaped by our childhood experiences. I remember that my mother had a book prominently displayed in our home.

When I say prominent, imagine the den (do homes even have those anymore?) where I watched television, played video games, and escaped to when my family's emotional temperature gauge was hitting red. In this so-called room of refuge, my mother kept the book *If Life Is a Bowl of Cherries: What Am I Doing in the Pits?* by Erma Bombeck.

I've come to learn of the cult following this book has, but at the time, and even now when I reflect on the book's cover image, all I remember is the stomach-turning shame I felt. My life, or that of my family, was so unbearable that they actually had a book written about us. Now, of course, I know Bombeck wasn't a family friend or acquaintance. But her book was one of the first indicators to me that love and family can be fickle, contrary to what Hollywood would have us believe, and that might just be okay.

The book, however, functioned like a secret code—it was only embossed on the cover, yet my mother and anyone else never whispered it into existence. It served as a silent reminder, a quiet shame, that the family story I'd dreamed of wasn't in the cards.

We must understand the power of holding two truths simultaneously to comprehend the magnitude and value of the stories that define us. I can honor the good, the bad, the ugly, and the discombobulated nature of my upbringing, and still recognize the less-than-favorable experiences I struggle to shake all these years later. Storytelling is never about self-selecting; it is about the perceived good we choose to display publicly, as many of us have seen on Facebook and other social platforms. Nobody is genuinely that "in love" or happy, but they did have 2.5 seconds to smile for a selfie or family photo.

As I grappled with the loss of a company I had built, solely because I had no other options after losing my job, I often thought about Erma Bombeck's book. I felt shame for my perceived failure and struggled to maintain the love I had for the pain, sweat, and tears I had invested in the effort.

The value of understanding the impact and role of shame in my defeat (not failure) has helped me reconcile the love I experienced during the good times. I am now better prepared to discuss my full-throated entrepreneurial journey because I have embraced my love and appreciation for my contributions, allowing them to exist in plain sight, much like a certain book that overshadowed any affection I might have had for cherries.

I will never understand why my mother thought it was a good idea to share her emotional struggles with the rest of the family. It serves as a reminder that the stories that define us are likely to always have a bit of tarnish.

Double Wide Smiles

My children and the famous people I interview often remind me that my idea of being cool is just that—mine. A couple of years ago, I was asked about interviewing the Red Rocket, Sammy Hagar of Van Halen fame. He is a musical icon by any measure, enduring past the heyday of a life lived out loud. How on earth can anyone prepare to capture even a glimpse of a rock star's story? Before I allowed myself to slide down a path of uncertainty, I dipped into the spring that has served me well for years—when in doubt, look for the proposed minor detail to see if there is a narrative rainbow at the end.

I am not musical, so I was not going to interview Sammy about music specifically. I navigated through all the expected topics about living a rock star life and zeroed in on life before explosive stages and bottles of excess. Beneath the surface, I discovered a family history rich in want yet lacking in means. That was the key, I thought, as I began to map out my approach to the interview. I wouldn't ask Sammy about music; I'd focus on Sammy being himself.

Sammy could not have been a more engaging interview subject—kind in his eyes and thoughtful with his ears. Interviews can feel off-kilter when the interviewee's preparation focuses on bullet points and catchy lines crafted not from their experiences but rather from well-meaning public relations and publicity professionals. And here's a little secret for all the leaders seeking to understand the stories of those they hope will join them on their professional mission: genuine interest in someone's "why" and the origin of that "why" creates the lasting bonds necessary for forging trusting relationships.

Thankfully, I followed my own advice, focusing on everything from Sammy's philanthropic efforts to the lettuce fields of California that supported a family's dream. I discovered that Sammy's ability to unleash all of his senses upon adoring fans was rooted in his experiences in those lettuce fields.

Known for leaving it all on stage every night, Sammy, in turn, unwrapped vivid detail after vivid detail of the boy he once was, the grandfather who lived in a double-wide trailer, and the world he created for Sammy through his love of Italian food. The aroma of his grandfather's cooking swirled through the trailer, out the front door, and across the landscape that Sammy's family shared with the lettuce they harvested.

As the sands of the interview dwindled, I engaged my reflective side and shared with Sammy that while he may have left the lettuce fields of California, those fields hadn't left him. I truly wanted him to know that, in the only way I could, I understood his story and respected the love he clearly still held for those days.

My experience with Sammy reminded me that sometimes the stories that define us are not necessarily those we are publicly known by.

Interview

Okay, so it's safe to say that you and I are not rock stars, unless you actually are a rock star. In that case, thank you for embodying the creative anthems of my life. For the rest of us who may be a bit reluctant to explore stories where love is not just an idea or the essence of a melody but rather a driving force behind our motivations, let's consider some key questions to ask ourselves in order to understand the role love plays in our ability to capture and tell better stories.

- **Who** impacts my story of love?
- **What** role do I play in stories with loved ones, romantic interests, colleagues, and friends?
- **Where** do I find love in my story?
- **When** does love impact my story positively or negatively?
- **Why** do love stories always end in loss, regret, or failure?
- **When** to "call it"—understanding the love of a story can *end* a story.
- **Can** love stories endure, and how can I adapt as the characters and scenes change?

The answers are yours and yours alone. This isn't about crafting a love story, but it is about understanding our passions' role in the types of stories we tell and to which audiences we tell them. I received a phone call out of the blue from an advertising executive in New York. I knew the caller during a brief stint collaborating on a story and movie about gun violence threatening the lives of kids across Chicago. He was there when I interviewed the film's writer and star. I must have left an impression because the story I ultimately told was about the why of the filmmaker and the love he had for a subject rife with sadness and regret.

The ad executive chatted briefly about the movie and my story before revealing the real reason for his call—his agency was partnering with a new sports league affiliated with the UFC (mixed martial arts). The founder, Hall of Fame fighter Khabib Nurmagomedov, wanted to share his story. Before I realized it, I had been connected to a corporate marketing leader for the league. I had been in this situation before, metaphorically speaking, and understood the game I was entering. A series of expectations followed by rules and timelines that would limit any creative control I thought I had.

I knew nothing about mixed martial arts, but I was intrigued by a potential story that was unique in almost every way from what I had experienced. The league executive's cheerfulness suggested that I was possibly doing them a favor—a joyful position to be in, no matter your profession. I mentioned that I'd love to interview Khabib, but I wanted to conduct the interview in person and inside the octagon. I may not have been considered cool by famous fighter standards, but my love of storytelling pushed me to aggressive, creative levels I hadn't reached before.

After a series of hmms, the call ended. She said she would pitch the idea to Khabib and let me know. Minutes later, my phone rang, and it was an enthusiastic "Yes!" Of course, my to-do list quickly transformed into a list of don'ts from the league, but I didn't mind. I had the chance to spend time with and interview someone completely foreign to my life and experiences—a dream scenario where the script has yet to be written.

My idea had clearly spread because, as I was escorted into the arena, I met another writer from a different publication. This was fine with me, as I thought it meant everything would unfold as I had envisioned. As the crew set up the plush chairs inside the octagon, discussions started about who would interview Khabib. At first, my competitive side wanted to go first. Then, I realized a key part of finding the story was to let the environment help create experiences where stories have room to roam.

"He can go first. No problem."

I settled into a ringside seat to review my notes—one eye on my prep sheet and the other on the body language of Khabib and the "first" guy. For a brief moment, I closed my eyes, focusing on what they were saying. Then, I observed their interaction, letting their voices fade into gibberish. I wanted to grasp the stories being told and the love Khabib was either expressing about his story or keeping tucked away in the proverbial corner of the ring.

I was really glad that I kept my excitement in check during the interview. I could tell the reporter was concentrating on what I consider surface-level story elements, or what corporate communications offices might view as press release stories. The opportunity was there, and I was ready to seize it!

I entered the octagon with a man whom aficionados of the sport described as "terrifying" and began to connect with him, not just as a fighter. We talked about the impact retirement had on his psyche, his family's role in this next chapter of launching a league to compete against the UFC, and how his concept of home had changed over time. I focused on discovering what he loved about his story and how it might illuminate future paths. Khabib spoke of his homeland in Dagestan, a republic of Russia, and his desire to return to his village home to sell vegetables to his neighbors.

This is a true love story about an unsuspecting character, better known for battle than for community. I could have easily chosen to follow an editorial path focused solely on fighting techniques and memories of past triumphs. However, I would have missed an opportunity to convey a story that hadn't reached millions of fans.

Khabib unknowingly taught me a valuable lesson that day about storytelling: find angles that reveal why something matters to someone, rather than focusing on pursuits steeped in rote details and sterile recitations of missions and visions. Never underestimate the importance of actively considering the potential of a given story from both our perspective and that of a universal "other."

Love, as they say, is a two-way street. Storytelling about our love or passion for something or someone requires a thorough examination of the nature of love in the stories that define us.

A series of questions follow, presented in no particular order, that serve as a pretext for exploring stories that involve love. Read them. Reflect on different chapters of your life and consider how the outcomes might have changed if you had applied conscious thought to your perspective and their experience of your role.

"Our" Perspective:

- How much of my story is true?
- What story underscores my comprehension of what it means to be loved/to love?
- Is it love to edit stories from fact to fiction?
- Is it love when we join in others' stories?
- Has love been a co-author of your story, and if so, how?
- Do we love the created path or the undefined journey?
- If love is the summit, why is regret regularly on the path?
- Why is love important to our story?

- If losing love hurts, why do we often feel closer to our feelings in fallout?
- Love of and for others seems definable, if not rational; love of ourselves requires accepting our shortcomings and talents.
- Are our stories of ourselves authentic or driven by a need to protect?
- Can our stories be loving if our choices hurt others?
- When saying no actually represents loving ourselves.

"Their" Perspective:

- Are they a story-of-one, or are we co-authoring a new story together?
- Do they realize they always play the hero or victim in the story of us?
- Is this story their story or the company's?
- Is their vision love of the mission or objectively different?
- Do they realize they are being blindly led by love and not reality?

I could argue that my first love was sports—not just the games I played or the thrill of victory, but a specific team. The NBA's Detroit Pistons proudly earned the nickname "Bad Boys" during their back-to-back championships in the late 1980s and early 1990s. My hometown team meant everything to me then and still does now. I loved them through the heartbreaking and unforgettable moments of complete failure, and I celebrated "our" victories as triumphs over life's challenges.

I thought about them day and night—so much so that I plastered my bedroom ceiling with player posters, timeless front pages, and game memorabilia. My theory was that sleeping under the stars was one thing, but drifting off to sleep beneath the headlines of greatness was a stroke of genius. Even as I pinball through middle age, the bell of my Pistons love still rings true to this day.

Love and stories are symbiotic. We can choose to embrace origin stories filled with the notion of love or remain steadfast in the belief that our interests will always lie in data, press releases, and results. After plenty of "why," I'm happy to get to the "what."

What say you?

Free love needed. Prices may vary.

3 | Neighborly Stories

Converting Envy into Appreciation

Ignore destiny and flirt with punctuation.

Recognition is a curious concept. Many of us, deep down, where the cobwebs weave through our memories, yearn for acknowledgment and have since we realized the power of cause and effect. It is only in adulthood that we develop a deeper and more meaningful understanding of what it means to be recognized.

Sometimes, we long for recognition from our friends and family for the accomplishments we have poured our heart and soul into. When the other end of the line is silent, we withdraw at the thought of an achievement missing its moment.

Why?

We are human, and we live, work, and form friendships and pursue hobbies with people and activities where our contributions are recognized and appreciated. However, like any report card experience, the outlier often creates tension—the grade that doesn't reflect the entirety of our work or the presentation that fell short. For this reason, we develop what I call *Side Stories*.

Side Stories are the off- and on-ramps that either divert our current trajectory to a more agreeable destination or guide us back to the most familiar narrative. When I wrote for *Forbes*, I recall the motto, "Stay in your lane," which means to write about what you know and where you have expertise.

Life isn't nearly that clear-cut.

Side Stories can feel like a piece of mid-afternoon candy when things aren't going your way—a little boost. Our only responsibility is to recognize *them* for what they are and the role they play in helping us understand the world's impact on us.

We often notice others' *Side Stories* when we look at our phones. If you scroll through any social platform, you'll likely see updates from friends that are really *Side Stories*. I argue that many of us are probably better at recognizing the *Side Stories* of our colleagues, friends, and family than we are at identifying our own now.

Stack up these moments through the narrative of window shopping, and envy creeps in—that feeling that the all-encompassing other is doing better or more than you and me. Sure, if we're honest, envy has a place in the human experience. Envy can spur action in various human-centric activities, such as relationship courting, job hunting, hobby seeking, and many more instances where envy ignites our competitive fire within ourselves.

The trick. Yes, there's a trick—nothing deceptive, but a conscious effort to identify the stories in the room, whether digital or otherwise. When we commit to recognizing the impact of others' stories on our perception of our own, we can understand how we want our next chapter to unfold. We can't just react for the sake of reacting. We need to grasp our character in our story and the influences, whether controlled or not, that color the narrative we create.

Those who have followed my storytelling journey know how impactful my African explorations have been for my spirit. As we approached Dakar, Senegal, I had a candid discussion with myself—indeed, I pulled the various *Side Stories* in my mind into one cohesive edition to evaluate the stories I wanted to share ... that I needed to share. I was guilty of window shopping other storytellers' approaches, and often, the result of these quick glimpses was dry and frankly dull text.

As we softly landed, I looked down at the dry, pale palette of the Western African landscape and realized I was writing someone else's story—not mine. I was too focused on editors and creative collaborators telling me what to do, while my narrative vehicle swerved in and out of oncoming traffic. At that moment, I committed myself to writing with feeling, emotion, and wonder.

I still find myself looking at others' work, but now I'm *window shopping* for a different reason—inspiration! It may have taken me more than four decades to realize that I have been my own worst critic. To think otherwise would grant power to the editors in our lives who keep us confined to our designated lanes, not out of concern but out of a need to contain their anxieties about the how, what, where, when, and why of their lives.

As we journey through the pages of this book, we will revisit many of my travels in Africa, including cascading down the Nile River over crocodile-infested waters, safaris in Tanzania, and puddle-jumper flights at the base of Kilimanjaro.

I want to take you off the beaten path and into a story that highlights the importance of recognizing the power of editing our approach to the characters we portray in our own narratives. At times, we serve as the *Side Story* in someone else's tale. Other times, we are the mid-afternoon candy when they seek inspiration. Great stories come from great storytellers who understand the greatness of their audiences.

Shortly after my adventures learning about the dangers of child marriage in West Africa and the efforts to combat the generational theft of one's future, I received an invitation to travel to East Africa with an NGO (non-governmental organization) called Pangea to explore the origins of storytelling within a refugee camp.

A journey filled with lesson after lesson about living life without the advantages of time offered perspective and served as the foundation for my TEDx Talk. It was quite an adventure to write my TEDx Talk from the banks of the Nile River and later record it for organizers from inside my hut late at night deep within the camp. While I was in my moment, others were watching without notice.

The organizers of Pangea, who have become dear friends, acknowledged my awe at the nightly communal campfires, where locals shared generational stories in their native language for Westerners to experience. There may be seven Wonders of the World, but I would argue that this experience is more than just a bucket list item for anyone curious about the origins of our species.

Months went by, and we all returned to the comforts of our Western lives when I received a call from Pangea. They announced their first International Prize for Literacy, and I was the recipient.

I was recognized not for something I produced, but for my approach and sensitivity to the power of words and stories in improving the lives of others. The organizers were aware of my advocacy work in Nashville, focusing on removing the misdeeds of book-banners from schools across the state.

The experience taught me a valuable lesson about the power of knowing your lane—not necessarily staying in that lane, but understanding that my own story, filled with missteps and achievements, serves a purpose for others. It was a profound lesson about finding dignity in our stories and the impact *Side Stories* can have on our perspective and that of those in the shadows.

I shared my acceptance speech exactly as it is because it underscores the significance of *Side Stories* in the larger narrative of our lives.

Let me take you into a Chicago hotel's ballroom …

★ ★ ★

Imagine a brisk November night on the outskirts of Chicago. Most attendees know each other, and greetings of familiar chatter fill the air between finger foods and the clinking of glassware. I feel like a one-of-a-kind, not because I hold a special title, but because my story, which I will share, is personal. It means a great deal to me, and I only hope that the conclusion of my remarks reflects similar looks of acceptance and approval that I'm seeing at the beginning of the evening.

Besides my fraying nerves, I wonder if my tone will fit the moment and the audience. I can barely eat and worry that my glass should be filled with water instead of high-octane banquet booze. I find comfort in the purpose of my remarks and in the people and places that represent the rhythm of my speech. I can feel the space between my neck and the oxygen-tight collar of my dress shirt getting damper. I'm used to capturing the stories of others … not sharing my own.

As the moment of introduction approaches, I feel a second wind propelling the sails of representation, not accolades. One last swig of water … "Please welcome our recipient …"

Time to make my friends, who are in different time zones, proud …

I'm a dad. I have a 9-year-old daughter and an 11-year-old boy. I drive them to school every day. It's a time for randomness to take center stage. They want to talk about school, friends, politics, yes politics, why we have war, why moms and dads sometimes argue, and whether I have everything prepared for their soccer practice and after-school activities. Today was a bit different. They both were very curious about the award Daddy was receiving.

My daughter surmised that I was basically winning a Grammy Award, insert laughter.

I talked with my children about how life for other children around the world can be very, very different from what they know and experience. We talked about my trip to Africa with Pangea, my advocacy work to support librarians, school boards, and literacy companies battling extreme positions.

The doors closed as we said our goodbyes, giving me time to meander through Nashville traffic on my way to the airport while reflecting on our conversation. I'm proud that my children are curious. That they question the immediate world around them.

And then I think about the door to life that I have been blessed to have access to. How the locks of life simply pivot from left to right, opening doors of opportunity, sometimes in excess, but always laden with an expectation that they will open based on countless experiences of the past.

Many of the doors that have been unlocked
for me have come through hard work, yes,
hopefully through a delicate balance of
individualism and collective opportunity.
They've also opened for me because of the
longitude and latitude that define my
existence. And when those coordinates
shift, through the power of travel,
I am reminded of my opportunity.

So, whether I'm on the Kenyan border with
WaterAid documenting water insecurity or
hanging out with our own Drew Edwards,
the Pope, and United Nations officials in Rome,
I am reminded of the responsibility to attend to
the smallest elements of life, those powerful
experiences and reminders of who we are and
the impact we can have around the world.

I am a lucky man.

I am the son of my late father, who was once a
boy struggling to survive in war-torn Germany
during the Second World War. I was raised by a
man who struggled to celebrate life only one step
removed from the atrocities and residue of war.

*I was raised by a man who taught me the
power of language, the nuance of propaganda,
and the necessity to honor the subtleties of life
that define people, cultures, and distant lands.*

I am a lucky man.

*So, when I embarked on three separate
adventures across the African continent over
the last 18 months, I thought of my
late father … trying desperately to think
about those I might learn from, laugh with,
and share commonalities with, even if
our skin color differed, our sense of safety
and security, and our general understanding
of our individual purposes differed.*

*I think of work being done in Western Africa
to empower young girls that I witnessed to
support a life of autonomy and independent
mind, free to interpret the world without fear
of child marriage or a life spelled out in
limiting and prescribed roles.*

*Young women who learn to farm the land
and harvest information from books and
experiences. The brand of information that
frees one's mind to make choices and
decisions supporting a life of substance,
health, and agency. A life jumpstarted
through the power of education and the
application of words.*

A life forged in the tenets of knowledge.

A life lived beyond words.

*I think of my previous life in mental health
and the countless families struggling to interpret
the life and needs of a child with autism.
The power of language, spoken and
unspoken, and the unlocking nature of
a moment shared.*

*I think of the citizens of this country who call
Skid Row in Los Angeles home. Those that
I worked with to find meaning and definition
in personal stories of chaos, confusion, and
isolation— isolation from the mere comprehension
of individualized healthcare options.*

Small alterations profoundly impact souls living on the outskirts of society.

A life lived beyond words.

Every time I slink down the steps of news updates reminding me of the chaos around us, I pause. I think about generations past and what they might think about a world in 2023 that is defined more by our differences than by the genetic code of connection … we all share.

Are the troubles we face any more daunting than those of past generations?

Sadly, I live in a state that openly prides itself on banning books that tell the story of Ruby Bridges, books that invoke the teachings of Martin Luther King Jr.

And, yes, I have stumbled into being what I call an Accidental Advocate … speaking on the capitol steps in Nashville in support of equitable access to books, crafting strategic

*messaging for media in an attempt to push back
against the ban of digital libraries that inhibit
children of all ages and needs from the wonder
of books ... of story.*

*It is easy to think of literacy as the ability to
read the words in front of us with context and
understanding of the emotions displayed
through rich and poetic verse.*

*Literacy, in truth, unlocks the door to life,
to a sense of agency, allowing for the beauty
of life to unfurl. We are all here tonight
because we all support a literate society;
we love the spirit, grit, and determination
of the incredible human beings behind the
fingertips of the Pangea logo.*

*We're also here because each one of us, deep
down, knows that a life without keys to the
door of opportunity puts us at risk of living a
life stunted, behind the walls of oppression, food
insecurity, inadequate healthcare, gender
inequality, and education steeped in cultural
maintenance rather than inspiration, let alone
personalization.*

It is an honor to be the first recipient of the Pangea Prize for Literacy. I humbly accept this honor, but I share it with my friends here and abroad who approach life not as a series of accomplishments recorded by the acquisition of currency but by the experiences, translatable in any language, that accurately depict the human experience, the struggle, the sacrifice, joy, and exuberance for making a difference, one fellow human at a time.

Our impact can be felt across the kitchen table from classroom to classroom, here in the U.S. or under the African sun in Uganda.

The butterfly effect of transformational impact travels across the great lakes and over the ocean to continents far and wide. I believe we have a responsibility as collective owners … of the keys of opportunity to support efforts that strive to educate, with compassion and dignity for worlds and cultures, unlike our own, with a deep desire to embrace life through equitable learning opportunities.

The picture behind me. I am proud to say that I took that picture inside a classroom at the Imvepi Refugee Settlement. Every time I look at it, I feel a visceral pull to acknowledge these children and the power of curiosity, the power of "want," and the willingness to participate.

Like many of your children, my children thumb through countless books and resources daily. It's not their fault.

Words are everywhere for them.

Stories of great adventure, inspiration and tragedy, mystery, fairy princesses, and heroes. That isn't the case around the world.

It really hit home for me on my trip with Pangea. The school year was just starting, and walking down a red dirt road, there would be countless students of all ages laughing and smiling ... and carrying ONE book.

Their ONLY book.

The grip tight. The representation of ownership on full display.

A sense of pride.

And so, while we sit here tonight, in this beautiful room … just know that the world's future scientists, teachers, engineers, poets, caregivers, artists, writers, and innovators are clutching a single point of connection to the world.

It just might be their only one.

A book. A symbol of literacy that creates a relationship with dreams yet to be borne by the citizens of this planet. I will leave you with this … the letters we build into sentences turn into love poems and marriage proposals, birth announcements and graduation notices, new-found employment letters, and notes asking for forgiveness or assistance.

A literate world goes beyond words, painting a picture of access, equity, and most importantly … possibility.

I thank Pangea for this incredibly humbling honor. I thank all of you for living beyond the walls of your comfort and for participating in the wondrous pursuit of a literate world.

Literacy is the key

The door, I contend, is right in front of us ...

To a world ... beyond words.

Thank You!

The breath of completion filled my nose, triggering a full-body sensation of relief. Who knew that words, and the sharing of words and stories, could be so exhausting? A series of *Side Stories* for the audience to reflect on ... core stories for me to immerse myself in.

Interview

I can't fully grasp the impact of my speech on the attendees at the event on the outskirts of Chicago that early winter evening. However, I can convey the profound appreciation and sense of representation I felt that night. The festivities weren't about me; rather, they celebrated those who inspired all of us with their grace, vulnerability, and stories to share.

I strive to share this level of openness with interview subjects to authentically understand their stories. I can laugh or at least shrug at the tales shared with me after interviews with CEOs, investors, and cultural changemakers, who often wanted to hear the behind-the-scenes stories of those I had previously interviewed.

The first time this happened, I remember feeling a bit stunned. The person before me had achieved a great deal; all they wanted to know about was the last person I interviewed. Soon, I began to expect similar interactions with guests after their interviews with me. If I turn the coin over, I think about those who, before the interview, would doubt whether they could "match" wits with previous and publicly notable guests. The aw-shucks of it all similarly surprised me, just like those who wanted to know secrets at the conclusion of my interview.

The lesson for me is that the perspective we take and the stories we fawn over, ridicule, avoid, or cling to are akin to genres in music, television, and movies. If I struggle to grasp the essence of another person's story, I miss the chance to connect with them through new and diverse life experiences. Additionally, I risk coming across as contextually tone-deaf.

To combat this unfortunate outcome in the stories we aim to tell, it can be beneficial to understand our responses to the following questions:

- When should my story take center stage?
- Is it appropriate to tell stories that compare my or our accomplishments to others?
- What story can I tell that conveys an understanding of the narratives surrounding me and how they influence my decisions?

It takes great restraint to prioritize others' stories over our own. Yet, this expression of narrative deferment sets the pace and charts the path forward for those you aim to positively influence. If I interview you and ask about the reasons behind your professional pursuits, will you be able to resist the temptation to embellish or highlight your market prowess? Can you embrace authentic storytelling that reveals the accomplishments within your efforts and your company, or will you lean toward comparing the achievements or setbacks of your direct competition?

As you reflect on your suggested responses, examine how the successes or failures of others have affected your life. How have you generally reacted, and how could you respond upon recognizing the compelling nature of your "neighbor's" story?

★ ★ ★

I was a pretty typical boy growing up—sports, competition, girls, and school dominated my life. I cared about what others thought of me, fighting tooth and nail to hide my desires. Walking to and from class offered plenty of chances to manage my teenage fears, many of which were sweat-induced and self-inflicted worries about others who likely struggled to fit in just like I did. It's clear to me that, at that time and understandably so, I didn't value the story I was starting to tell.

If we translate that coming-of-age story to our initial days on a college campus or our first job interview, we've all likely found ourselves in similar situations, comparing our perceived shortcomings to those flaunting their answers. Perhaps we shouldn't wish away such challenging experiences or hope that our children, friends, or neighbors can avoid such harsh human realities.

But wait!

What if we could fully understand the impact of stories written by others on our self-perception and the narratives we aspire to share? Perhaps we could turn the dilemma around to consider it from a different perspective.

Is it possible to view the stories others are writing without judging or pretending about our own narratives? I'm optimistic. I believe we all have the chance to think more deeply about the stories we observe from others and reassess the value we assign to our process of crafting stories that reflect our lives.

Considerations

- We need to understand how to diagnose our role in the narratives we believe we know about our neighbors.
- The strength of pausing our narrative to make space for the narratives of others.
- Stories can serve as a powerful social equalizer. How can we reshape our narrative to resonate with our neighbors' authentic experiences?

The world continues to shrink as the bridges of technology expand. The concept of neighbors has evolved from just down the street to around the globe. As you reflect on the type of storyteller you'd like to be, remember the importance of transforming your adversaries or competitors into neighbors—your stories will naturally forge a connection where envy or resentment once existed.

I may not have ever lived in an African village, but communal approaches to storytelling enlightened my perspective to be compassionate where I was once comparative.

Read a room. Tell a story.

4 | Negotiating Life

The Role of Conflict in Our Stories

Fear not. Tomorrow arrives after today.

"As a man, as a guy, a boy, it's not normal to talk about these things [failures] and talk about feelings. You don't want to show weakness, and you don't want to be a burden to your family and your company.

"So what do you do?

"You keep things inside. You try to hide them. In 2022, we went from 250 to over 500 employees. I lost my father. It was completely chaotic and I couldn't get enough oxygen to my brain."

—Jonas Helmikstøl

The sweat was beading up on both of our hairlines. I was stressed that I would somehow fail him, and I knew he was nervous about sharing his authentic and raw story with a live audience of the most influential European climate-tech investors.

It felt like we were going on stage together.

Usually, I get on stage and feel a clear, natural distinction between myself and the guests accompanying me. However, this experience felt different. There seemed to be a lot at stake, even though I wasn't aware of the specifics. I had met him just a day earlier on a park bench by a central fountain beneath the shadow of historic Norwegian architecture. I liked him. He was honest and straightforward, requiring very little prompting or probing. We discussed the essence of the event scheduled for the following day and even drifted into personal stories and shared experiences as fathers.

There was one significant difference: I took a calculated risk. I broke the *fourth wall*—the invisible barrier between actors and the audience. I set aside any division between church and state while interviewing him as a guest. Something within me suggested that revealing part of my own story would encourage him to share his. It was simply a matter of joining Jonas in the revelatory spirit he demonstrated.

Law of the Land

A few years ago, I found myself in the office of Giovanni Fili, the Swedish founder and CEO of Exeger, conducting an in-depth interview for a profile piece in *Forbes*. At that time, Fili shared with me, "I live my life like a shark. My philosophy is that if I stop moving, I die. I will suffocate like a shark." I recognized this kind of confidence, which felt distinctly American. The interview spanned a variety of topics and remains one of my favorite in-person interviews. His commitment to sustainability and energy inspired me, and we bonded over our shared dreams to make a difference.

It was evident that we connected, and today, I consider Giovanni a dear friend, someone I've met several times since that first interview.

What I didn't know was that the lesson from that experience came only after the mics were "cold." After the interview, while I gathered my belongings, we found ourselves discussing his "next" and the opportunities to share his story broadly. He hesitated. He flinched. This wasn't the "shark" I had seen just an hour earlier.

I clearly missed something: a context for the Nordics and the public expression—or lack thereof—of achievement.

That was the first time I had heard the term *Jantelagen.* Giovanni explained that it is a "law" that governs the region as a way of being, acting, and reacting to those in one's community (more on this later). Giovanni was that "shark." He was just a shark in his ferocious approach to building the best company he could—this wasn't my version of the ABC hit show *Shark Tank,* where boasting about accomplishments is the name of the game and attracts investment.

It all started to make sense to me—the luminaries, rock stars, and famous entrepreneurs I had encountered in the region all appeared to be averse to self-promotion. At first, this was a romantic idea, as I pondered a world where professional deference was the norm rather than the bold proclamations that typically set the tone in America.

I observed the hidden toll of suppressing emotions related to pain, triumph, and similar experiences, which bear a heavy burden.

Context Makes the World Quiet Down

I have come to understand the culturally embedded nature of the *Law of Jante*—known as *Janteloven* in both Danish and Norwegian, *Jantalagen* in Swedish, *Jante laki* in Finnish, and

Jantelögin in Icelandic. The Danish-Norwegian author Askel Sandemose (1899–1965) introduced the concept of Janteloven in his 1933 book *A Fugitive Crosses His Tracks* (*En Flyktning Krysser Sitt Spor*). The book depicts the story of a fictional Danish town, Jante, where all citizens relinquish their identities to the community.

I speak from experience that Sandemose's law still lives on, for better or worse, as the world shrinks and capitalism rises. Imagine the Ten Laws (as follows) within an American context and think about how your portrayal of your accomplishments might require negotiation to meet the tenets of the fabled writer.

The Ten Laws of Jante

1. Do not think you are anything special.
2. Do not think you are as good as we are.
3. Do not think you are smarter than we are.
4. Do not imagine yourself better than we are.
5. Do not think you know more than we do.
6. Do not think you are more important than we are.
7. Do not think you are good at anything.
8. Do not laugh at us.
9. Do not think anyone cares about you.
10. Do not think you can teach us anything.

The fourth wall began to fall, and I told Jonas that I knew what he was talking about—that I really knew about the impact external pressures can have on one's psyche. With the metaphorical wall at my feet, I shared summaries of my company's death and the slow death I had personally experienced in the aftermath. Jonas didn't have to say anything, but he did, sharing, "*You understand me.*"

The energy we generated on that late Sunday afternoon in Oslo carried over to the next day as we waited backstage at the renowned Startup Lab's Climate Tech Summit. A theater-in-the-round setting provided the ideal Shakespearean backdrop to unveil the results of Jonas's journey from national hero to an entrepreneurial *leper* of sorts.

Introductions were made, and we ascended the stage to delve into the rise-and-fall story of *Easee*, the innovative Norwegian EV (electric vehicle) that flirted with unicorn status, only to narrowly avoid bankruptcy, and the man behind it all.

The law of Jante was temporarily suspended by a *court* of two dads oceans apart. They recognized in one another the negotiated price of entry to an authentic story that needed to be told.

Rod: *Did you struggle to separate yourself from the company, from the expectations?*

Jonas: *We made a lot of money back then. It was successful, blah blah blah—billionaire, billionaire. The money gets a lot of attention, but people overlook what's happening at home. When you're sitting on the couch filled with anxiety, afraid of everything that could go wrong, there are countless emails and people trying to reach you.*

It never ends.

It's really overwhelming, and you don't want to disappoint anyone. I know I'm a people pleaser, and I think most of us are because we seek acceptance. We don't want to let others down. However, these pressures are quite challenging. These are the things I'm still trying to let go of because I still experience PTSD reactions.

This is especially true in the media because not everyone is as nice as you; they just want to make headlines, but they don't understand the impact of that pressure on a person.

> *When you fear going to the store, you fear just sitting on the couch—the phone rings, you get startled, and you feel these emotional punches in your stomach.*
>
> *This cannot continue. I know that many people around here know what I'm talking about.*

Rod: *I can see it in your physical reaction, those sitting close like it's bubbling up in you now.*

Against the cultural norms of Janteloven, Jonas responded, acknowledging that just the week prior, he had suffered a panic attack. You could hear a pin drop in the audience. I later learned from audience members that they were riveted because of Jonas's courage to speak in the first person, across the spectrum of human emotion, in a manner unaccustomed to the region.

Within weeks of our live event, I powered on my laptop and opened LinkedIn. Right in front of me, in what looked like bright neon lettering, was an announcement by Jonas that he secured investment for his current ventures.

I felt proud—not that Jonas needed my approval—because it was clear that the overwhelmingly positive response to our event changed the narrative most had set aside: that Jonas was the main character in the downfall of his company. On his own initiative, Jonas negotiated a truce that day between what was expected and his truth, navigating conflict to reveal a bright horizon toward the future.

Courting a Narrative

My company slipped through my fingers faster than I realized at the time. A brisk, cleansing north wind freed me from the solid yellow lines that divided the roadways into the suddenness— the rude awakening of bookies' stares. I have never formally gambled or even participated in fantasy sports leagues. However, I have gambled on the margins of dreams and paid a hefty toll as they withered away. The letter I wrote to myself helped me plant a flag that I mattered throughout it all, and my experience was real.

It (the letter in Chapter 2) also served as my "co-counsel" when losing the company was only the beginning.

My family had just rushed out for a day of errands, and I went to the gym for a quick workout. It was one of those days that just flew by for all of us. Shortly after, I returned home and, as usual, glanced toward the front door as I prepared to turn left into the driveway. Amazon boxes seemed to dominate the space on the front porch, and I had been trained to keep a watchful eye on everything.

I saw something—something yellow affixed to the doorknob. It was probably a business card from a roofing company or a plumber. As I ping-ponged up the stairs of the garage, I gave the solicitation little thought. I was listening to a sports interview on my phone, as usual, while cracking my post-workout eggs and remembering to take down whatever was at the door.

You know that feeling you get before the end is revealed—that unmistakably human ability to sense when the universe is taking a day off from protecting you? It was a notice, not a solicitation from the local sheriff's office—I was to be served by the court system.

I panicked. "Another one!" I couldn't believe that after all these years since my company was taken from me, I was still dealing with the fallout from a deeply disturbed individual who had outright slaughtered the financial well-being of countless other entrepreneurs. I couldn't share this with my wife or anyone else. I silently pleaded with the universe, hoping it was just a mistake. I called the number on the notice, and a patrolman answered and kindly said he'd return to my home to deliver the summons.

I didn't know what was coming, but I hoped my family wouldn't come home and that my neighbors wouldn't see. The patrol car pulled into the driveway, and the officer said, "I'm sorry I have to do this, sir." I told him it wasn't his fault; he was just doing his job. I signed on the dotted line, effectively setting the next six months of my life into motion.

I watched him pull out of the neighborhood. My family was still out and about, so I could sit and read what was being claimed against me. Taking a deep, exhaustive breath helped my hands unclasp the manila envelope. It was similar to previous complaints—this time, a lender my former business partner had defaulted on. He had pointed everything at me from the same playbook he used on others who had become friends through our shared stories of trauma.

I decided then and there that I would fight this claim with gusto and, most importantly, on my own and in secrecy! I learned a great deal about my story, the stories we are told in malice, and the influence that words and presentations can have on outcomes, even in judicial settings. The first time this happened, I thought my life was over. I consulted lawyers, but in the end, I realized I was better off fighting my own battle—I knew how to sleuth information, sequence stories, and advocate for a just conclusion. This time, though, I'd have to accomplish the feat in the middle of the night when my family's shadows were sound asleep.

Months passed as I followed the general path along the river of deep disappointment in our system, in my judgment, and the isolation I felt while staring at calendar dates, filled with a sense of impending doom. There were small victories along this river of pain, including a scheduling snafu at the court that allowed me to choose a date when my family would be out of town. I could put on my suit, head into court, and do so without hastily changing in the front seat of my car to avoid drawing suspicion. I could be my best self in the battle to save my financial future.

The most taxing part of the monthly pre-game process was thinking through contingencies so that I had well-thought-out responses to the plaintiff's counsel and the court writ large. If this happens, then this is the proof I'll submit. Should I file motions prior to the hearing to send a message that I wouldn't lay down and die? I mapped everything out. If I was going down, it wouldn't be because I lost my voice or belief in the rule of law.

★ ★ ★

As Y2K approached, the year 2000 for those who have forgotten about a time when we feared the power of the number 0 on the technologies and infrastructure managing our lives, I participated in a time-honored tradition for those in their 20s—traffic court. I had been caught going 45 m.p.h. in a 35 m.p.h. zone in Los Angeles. I know, most of you are probably thinking, I'll never drive with that guy. I concede that it (the event) deserves a bit of sarcasm. I had the option of either just paying the ticket and attending traffic school or contesting the violation in court. Well, I was young and full of my own ego, with some to spare, and I said, "Hell yes, I'll go to court!"

Cue a humbling moment.

I went to traffic court with hundreds of others that day. It ended in about five minutes. The judge told the crowd—yes, a crowd of defendants—that we each had one chance and one chance only. If we didn't accept the ticket, we would face additional punishment. I thought, "How outrageous!" If I had any sense, I'd just say yes per his instructions about accepting the ticket as he rattled through the names. A concert of yeses rang out as each name was crossed off his list. I noticed that the motorcycle cop who pulled me over was in attendance, so I knew I was dead to rights, as they say.

I told myself that day that I would never go through that experience again—I'd be prepared on the off chance I'd be back.

★ ★ ★

Advocate

Advocating for myself hasn't always been easy—collateral damage from living under the stern thumb of a strong-willed father—largely due to my struggle to find my own voice. Recognizing that same challenge in others felt very natural. I leveraged this talent to my advantage as a storyteller in various fields, including media, mental health, technology, healthcare, and corporate positions.

I've advocated for various causes, regardless of whether I was directly affected, without needing to negotiate my own needs in the efforts I undertook. As my storytelling accompanied long flights to distant lands, I discovered other advocating voices that inspired my understanding of what it truly means to find one's voice, free from bias toward the agendas of others.

Abbe Ibrahim, the founder of the Operakällaren Foundation in Stockholm, Sweden, was born on the African continent but raised in the opulence of the queen city of the Nordics, at least among those he worked for. Abbe's story mirrors many American dream narratives—beginning under humble circumstances and leaky roofs, he worked as a dishwasher to make ends meet. He dedicated himself to his work, eventually achieving the position of CEO for AB Operakällaren, a restaurant and entertainment group at the pinnacle of society.

I've traveled with Abbe to Africa on two occasions to document stories of water insecurity that his foundation (co-founded by Thony Andersson) has worked to improve through partnerships with WaterAid. Abbe spent years adapting his African "voice" to Nordic ways and culture, only to discover his purpose back on the "continent." The following is an excerpt from an on-camera interview we conducted while walking across school grounds in a village in Uganda. Notice the approach he takes to the sequence of questions, literally moving from beneath his feet to the top of his imagination, navigating two worlds—one of opulence and the other of struggle.

Rod: *Do you feel at home back on the continent? What sights or smells are you connecting with that I am not?*

Abbe: *The first thing you notice is the red soil. It has a special flavor because you can actually eat it.*

You can actually eat it, not in a volume, but you can actually eat it because it contains a lot of minerals.

This is one of those memories that you remember as a child, the red soil. So, yes, I feel like I'm home. I feel like I am in a place where I feel confident. And I'm melting (emotionally), which I don't always do in Stockholm.

I love being here.

Rod: *Explain that feeling. Your body changes when you say love.*

Abbe: *The minute that I landed at the airport, the minute that we arrived in the bush—it's a relief.*

The air. You breathe easier. My system opens up.

I feel more like a human being.

Rod: *Talk about the moment when you first even thought about a foundation.*

Abbe: *It all started when I was on a trip to Kenya. We were privileged to visit a local village. The chief and a mother with* *a small infant welcomed us to the village. An hour later, when we left the village, that infant died.*

The cause of the death was lack of water.

This is how it started. We went back to Stockholm, and I founded the Operakällaren Foundation.

The mission is to provide people, whenever we can, however we can ... with water and toilets. We take them for granted, but the absence of those two things will stop any society.

Just try for one day, not going to the bathroom, or just try one day, not drinking water. See how your body reacts.

Rod:　*This is personal for you.*

Abbe:　*It is personal. It is personal.*

And as a father ... when you see your own child suffering ... and you know you can help. Just imagine those mothers and fathers who have children and they cannot help because they don't have access to water.

The basic need of human life, water.

Water is life.

*Without water, **nothing**, **nothing**, **nothing** functions.*

Nothing lives.

It's impossible.

Abbe found his voice and navigated his perspective by temporarily returning to his roots and discarding The Law of Jante. This created an impactful story that was authentic to his experience and inclusive of the two worlds he calls home.

I was brought in to help capture the story that Abbe and the team had been crafting for years, symbolizing an evolution in how progress can be documented—connecting their respective stories to those in need. Months later, I presented the stories, including Abbe's, to Crown Princess Victoria of Sweden and several dignitaries. This circle of storytelling was captured through the eyes of those navigating external conflicts to uncover the moral of a much larger narrative.

★ ★ ★

If I were going to update the program of my life and successfully deflect judgment against myself in the local courthouse that adorns the southern town I call home, I'd have to negotiate a different agreement with myself—I wouldn't wait to be hit with metaphorical punches; I'd initiate contact. I called the courthouse to understand the procedural steps I was in for and developed a plan moving forward. I destroyed reams of blank paper with ink smudges and residue from pounding my pen in exaltation when I discovered a piece of evidence or a line of thinking that accurately and poignantly represented my voice and case.

The day arrived. Based on the morning's events, it was time to calm my inner voice and prepare for any number of contingencies. I found a parking spot directly outside the courthouse, and because I was early, I examined each entrant, wondering if they were my sparring partner (plaintiff's counsel). I wasn't sure if I'd seen the one, in which case I would be able to make a motion for dismissal.

Oh, I forgot to tell you—I decided to represent myself.

I must have looked like an attorney because when I entered the courthouse lobby with book boxes and my briefcase in hand, the security guards quipped, "… oh the boxes," as if to say, another lawyer with their boxes. They inadvertently let me through, thinking I was on their team. I should have noted that reaction in the moment because within the hour, that subtle nod would free me from the internal hell I had endured.

I found a seat in the back of the courtroom to scan the attendees and see if I could catch a glimpse of the woman who would speak against me. I knew her name from the summons and realized that many of them represented the same lenders, allowing them to handle several cases at once, even during the same session. I chose to sit in the last pew for dramatic effect; I suspected that bringing in boxes of evidence would send a message that I was not to be taken lightly and that I could represent myself.

My name was called, and as I stacked one book box atop another, I began walking toward the front of the courtroom. The judge audibly exclaimed, "Ohhhh, the boxes." The lawyer spun around and scrutinized me from head to toe (these cardboard structures housing stacks of evidence were making an impact).

"You know this isn't the hearing, sir? This is just to set the date if we can't reach an agreement today on the outstanding debt owed to the plaintiff."

"I know, your honor," I said confidently as I set the boxes to the side of the podium. The judge looked at me and said, "Should I presume you are representing yourself?"

"Yes, your honor."

"I wouldn't recommend it," the judge said with obvious disapproval. He glanced up at me again, as if granting me a moment of grace.

"Your Honor, if I may, I have been devastated by the fraud that has been committed against me, and I'm here representing my family and my livelihood. I have stacks of evidence …"

"… I see," said the judge, clearly exhausted by my position.

"… and I have witnesses, and I'm ready to file the following motions today, if the court permits, so that I can be on equal footing with counsel during our hearing."

We agreed on a date for the hearing because I was protesting the claim. I returned to the same seat and waited. I knew I would have to speak with opposing counsel to drive home the point that I was not negotiating a settlement but prepared to *fight*. The session concluded, and I waited just outside the courtroom doors for the attorney. She emerged after a few minutes, and I politely asked for a moment.

I used my love of questions to crack open the window of opportunity. "Have you been able to review the police report I filed or the correspondence I shared with the Secret Service or the FBI?"

"No," she said, looking perplexed and resigned to the fact that I would be a formidable challenge. She took my information, glanced down at the boxes again, and said that, in all likelihood, they would drop the case because they didn't have time to deal with a lengthy trial.

Weeks later, 72 hours before the court date, I received an email stating that they had, in fact, decided to drop the case against me, finding that my evidence supported my claim. Because of the parallel emotions and duration of the entire ordeal, the lessons I learned about the nature of storytelling to navigate conflict will be forever etched in my mind.

Conceptually Speaking

Maybe it isn't wise of me as a husband, but I've been known to tell my wife during difficult times that at least "we can say we are experiencing the full range of emotions (during this hard time)." The look returned to me typically signals that my timing could be improved but that the sentiment had been successfully delivered.

There have been plenty of times when my stories have begun from the bottom and others when I'm flying high from the top of the mountain. When they start from the top,

I'm afforded time to reflect on a successful mission, and when the opposite is true, I question the vision I set out for myself. Companies, organizations, athletic teams, and high-achieving sole proprietors set visions that inform missions, speaking truth to power and execution.

Great storytellers create visions for their audiences, understanding that storylines or missions only resonate when crafted authentically and aligned with the creators' sensibilities. It is essential to pressure-test your stories across all areas of life through these filters to genuinely portray the intended image:

- Concept of truth
- Perceptions of others
- The role of secrecy in our stories
- Crafting stories from the top ... and from the depths of life

Ignition Points

I became accustomed to fearing the front door of my house, the sound of the doorbell, and the ring of my cellphone. I bonded with Jonas over the same PTSD signs and symptoms, for different reasons, but nonetheless impactful to our respective stories. Some might call them reactionary and frenetic responses to a world seemingly out of control.

Others might ruminate on the ills that had befallen them at the hands of others. I've learned to identify these triggers when I share my story: "Why am I saying 'that' whenever this topic comes up? Am I advocating my position at the wrong place and time, or am I truly present with those around me?" It has taken me a long time to realize the power of these questions. I've transformed those relatively unplanned story blurts into the questions I ask others. If I feel or sense that they have experienced a similar narrative trauma where negotiation wasn't possible, then a thoughtful question is warranted.

Call it "reading the room" if you want. I'd like to think that I recognize the moments that ignite me and then wonder, "Hmm, I wonder if it did the same for them?" Imagine the shift in corporate communications during times of change and tumult if leaders paused for a second, thought about the visceral response they might have to change, and then sequenced that self-observation in the comments they made to the teams they lead.

Strengthening our storytelling skills to embrace the moments that shape our contributions should not overlook these essential starting points:

- Our response to the story we've been dropped into or defined by.
- Critiques can serve as pivotal moments in any storyline.
- Negotiating the narrative through our physical bodies— recognizing the significant signals that reveal the parts of the story we'd prefer to discard.

Perspective

I've said many times that I am actually the lucky one when I think about the work I've done. I have the distinct honor of collaborating with newsmakers, innovators, futurists, and changemakers from around the world, and yet, almost like clockwork, I conclude discussions thinking, "I just learned more about myself through the lens and perspective of their story, and they didn't even notice."

It serves as a subtle reminder for both of us that we ought to interview ourselves—asking challenging questions about who supports our stories. Isn't it reasonable to argue that we should be our most steadfast advocates for the lives we strive to lead?

- Why do we feel compelled to negotiate against our own interests in the story?
- Can we gain a clearer understanding of when and where we should advocate for our story or negotiate its relevance to a broader narrative?
- How can I satisfy my narrative desire when it often appears to come at the expense of those I love, work with, and care about?

There were many lonely nights when the weight of the legal pretzel I was entangled in wore me down. The story I had so passionately shared with the judge and anyone who could hear me that day in the courtroom felt fleeting as I awaited my fate. I constantly asked myself whether I should advocate or negotiate—one side stoic to prove my innocence, the other born out of sheer exhaustion for a story I felt wasn't heard. I'm thankful that I settled on the voice I found within me that said, "If I don't fight for my rights, then unsavory types will continue to take advantage of those less inclined to advocate for themselves."

My perspective changed when I incorporated the stories of others I had met along the way who had also fallen victim to the same charlatan as I had. I'd like to think I was flexing wisdom or at least maturity through difficult waters.

Caution

Maturity can be defined by a discrete reaction in the face of untold challenges or by a series of events and corresponding responses that provide us the opportunity to act comprehensively, with little to no ego, and without sacrificing others. The challenge of navigating one's life arises when that battle is internal, echoing within our own mind, while external feedback could greatly benefit us.

Let us tackle each *monkey bar* (the bulleted questions) that follow to align our approach to the stories within us and those approaching us. Each answer will fill our lungs with narrative courage for the next *bar*, and before we know it, we'll be closer to meeting the moments that present themselves. The purpose of these questions isn't to memorialize a single perspective; rather, it is to lay the groundwork for a journey of ongoing introspection aimed at winning more battles than we lose.

- How has conflict shaped the story of who I am today?
- When should I advocate for my narrative, and when should I negotiate?
- How do cultural influences either suppress or encourage authentic storytelling?
- How can authentically incorporating conflict strengthen rather than weaken my narrative?

Remember that owning your story is vitally important and representative of one's life. It is equally crucial to reflect on the conversations people have when we finish sharing stories across the domains we inhabit. Are we harsh? Are we intentionally intimidating because our stories often begin with a roll call of accomplishments or a preamble setting the stage for future exoneration from any ill will? These are important aspects to examine and negotiate with ourselves as we navigate the increasingly complex world around us.

Consider these questions as if someone were asking about **you**:

- Do they realize that they approach most interactions as if they are negotiations?

- Have they played the victim in the story more frequently than the hero?
- Why can't they recognize the value they contribute?

The ultimate test for all of us is to look in the mirror and reflect on the stories that define us, bring us closer to our truth, and expand our potential in this world through the origin stories that shape our first steps. You may not share your story on a stage like Jonas or create narratives across continents like Abbe, or even fight or advocate through story to preserve your name, but a time will come when you see …

Story acts as a mechanism to meet the moment, honor yourself and your journey, and advocate for the marginalized—whether it's you or others.

Today I rise. Tomorrow I soar.

5 | Alternate Endings

Magical Middles

Request perfection. Live in the middle.

Many moons ago, I threw my name in the hat of a local TEDx Talk. I could picture the aftermath of a successful Talk, but the path to getting there seemed littered with blinking neon question marks.

- Could I pull it off?
- Did I have a story worth telling?
- Would people care?
- Had I accumulated enough life lessons to be believable?

I wasn't entirely sure what my motives were for presenting a talk or whether they were driven by ego or purpose. Thankfully, for everyone involved, I was not selected that year. I felt crestfallen not because I would have to face the daunting task of creating 18 minutes of value, but out of concern over competition. I understand that now—I didn't realize it then.

My relationship with TED and TEDx Talks and the brand had been a mixed bag up to that point. I had interviewed the Head of TED, Chris Anderson, for a *Forbes* article, and I even had the incredible opportunity to interview the late Sir Ken Robinson in person, regarded by many as the man whose talk made TED.

If anything, I was deeply connected to the brand's fabric and the significance of a talk for those fortunate enough to give one. Whether on the grand TED stage or the derivative TEDx stage, those who could check the TED box of accomplishments understood that their talk would forever be their headline.

Fast-forward a few years to a second encounter with Sir Ken Robinson, where I spent an afternoon sipping wine with him and his wife. During that time, I came across Robinson's equivalent, a British guy named Richard Gerver. He is a former Head Teacher (the British term for school principal) in England, who rose to international fame as an author and speaker following his TED success. Richard and I quickly became good friends, having periodic Zoom calls—no agenda required.

On one occasion, in Atlanta, Georgia, our itineraries coincided, leading to an unplanned get-together. Being of German descent and sitting next to a Brit built like a rugby player, what else could we do but toast our proximity with a couple of pints? Besides the banter and the interludes of "Another round, please," we discussed Robinson, the power of TED, and the near-miss I had experienced. I'll never forget my dear friend's sage words:

> You can't exclusively think about life through the lens of a final chapter (TEDx Talk). Your story hasn't been written yet, and when it is, that's when you'll find the TED stage.

Richard's words offered relief to a tired dream that had yet to come true, for a reason. Little did I know that my time wouldn't arrive for almost a decade.

★ ★ ★

February 24, 2023 – Tampa, Florida – TEDx

Title: Story is Our Currency

Speaker: Rod Berger

"The world that you and I know, the history of our civilization, the basic understanding that we have of one another is forged in one universal truth, story. Story is about capturing a moment in time, an essence, and inviting an audience to a shared experience.

"It's story, not facts, that has led teams, secured partnerships in business and marriage, started wars, perpetuated isms, prevented treaties of compassion and collaboration amongst cultures of difference."

_____

_____

_____

_____

"Data may be the new oil characterized by ones and zeros, but I contend that the pixelated present is dotted with fantastical stories yet to be told. And as we let the fourth industrial revolution wash over us, our relationship between data and the soul of our stories is at battle. If currency is our story, do we have enough in our narrative to author generations moving forward?

"I contend: Yes.

"The question is this …

"When I sit down to interview you, what will you share that will connect us? Because I'll be curious. Are you embracing your own story at work and at home?

"And if not, why not?"

★ ★ ★

Depending on our objective, we choose to start stories at various points along the arc of the actual story. For dramatic purposes, we might lead with the ending to influence the beginning and the middle. The "How did we get here?" of an unapproving parent speaking to their child or a middle manager struggling to guide newcomers through mistake-prone onboarding activities.

I learned a great deal from the TED experience: thinking, pleading with the sky above for a narrative direction, editing, editing some more, and eventually finding peace in the story I eventually told. My North Star clustered around the people and places often on the margins who had little to no say in their origin stories and even less to say in the life scripts society had stamped as final.

★ ★ ★

I often viewed my work in mental health as a version of bumper bowling, where defined and prescriptive approaches dominated, providing sanity for the provider, the system, and hopefully the patient or client. In hindsight, I should have taken dubious notes to reference later when creating my TEDx Talk. Both arenas celebrate neatly crafted thematic bubbles of information, packaging the uniqueness of each bubble within the parameters of the day. I've never been a fan of confined spaces or confined thinkers, and so I've struggled along the spectrum of both endeavors to refine my modular thinking.

This was never more apparent than when I worked with kids and families. Like clockwork, families would enter therapy with unofficially assigned roles and corresponding storylines— not to explore with the therapist, but to report (more on that in later chapters). Brushing with a very broad and acknowledged brush of generalities, moms and dads, sometimes grandparents, and definitely social service representatives, would approach the work with pre-packaged narratives.

- The problem we are having with _____ is ...
- They have been given every opportunity to ...
- I or we know you'll understand our position Dr._____.
- They don't understand the consequences.
- You need to ...

The actual list might resemble biblical scrolls in tone and definitiveness. The challenge for me, right from the start, was to explore alternative endings to the "set in stone" presentations I frequently received out of the gate.

- Could there be a rational explanation?
- How could outcomes differ with changes to the characters?
- Does everyone want a different ending?

The last point was the first source of contention for me as I struggled to accept labeling young people as dysfunctional lemons of society. I inherently believed that we may not be able to change or erase our origin story, but with an awareness of our roles comes the ability to rewrite the middle chapters to alter the concluding chapters of one's life.

★ ★ ★

I recall that it was late in the afternoon when I welcomed a family of three into my office. The identified patient, or IP, was clear despite the paperwork handed to me by the mother. She and her husband were bringing their teenage son to me because his actions were intolerable. Initial sessions are meant to establish the parameters and expectations, from me to them and from them to me. A general airing of grievances was relatively automatic in these highly charged settings. Parents would begin by stating their case—often running down a mental and sometimes literal bullet list of erroneous and destructive behaviors. I would glance at the teenager, who often looked away or sank deeper into their chest cavity, using their rolled shoulders like barricades against the onslaught of verbal bullets.

The further we traveled through the story of how "bad" their child was, the more I felt aligned with the teen. On this day, the ember that lit the flame was the consistent use of curse words directed toward adults, especially teachers and anyone seen as an authority figure.

When Dad circled back to the original complaint, I knew the roundabout was complete.

"Thank you for your transparency, Mom and Dad. It is clear that your concerns are valid, and I recognize the angst you feel. If you wouldn't mind stepping out so that I can speak with your son, I would greatly appreciate it. Shouldn't take but just a few minutes," I said.

"You want us to step out?" questioned the mother.

"Yes," I replied.

If there ever was a way to communicate the love for a profession, it would be marked by this moment of riding the therapeutic elevator, stuck between two floors. In less than 30 seconds, I conveyed respect for the parents' position and plight while acknowledging the teenager's inalienable rights as well—even if I made mom and dad momentarily upset.

The goal of my time with their son wasn't to conduct a military-style after-action review of complaints. I just wanted us to face the same direction. Nothing more. Nothing less. We might be looking out over a desert of bad decisions, but we were going to forge ahead together. I acknowledged that cursing at teachers might not get him what he wanted and even shared a wry laugh. Before bringing Mom and Dad back into the room to discuss our plan ahead, I set aside my notebook and pen, placed my hands on my knees, looked up at the teen, and said:

> I like you. Sure, swearing at adults isn't the best thing, but that tells me you care enough to speak up for yourself. We can work on the art of subtlety. You've got a fire inside, and that tells me there's a lot of talent inside. Now, just follow my lead.

I stood up and walked to the door. I looked out at Mom and Dad, and they looked back as if to say, "You see what we're talking about, right?" I politely smiled and motioned for them to return to my office. The two well-intentioned parents took their seats on the couch, both upright, ready, it appeared, to be validated by their previous proclamations.

"I just have to say how much I like your son. Sure, there are some basic things we can work on to avoid making the whole world mad at him, but there is something special about him, a fire, that I see, and I'm excited to work with him," I said.

At this point, you would think I had just reported a death to the parents, as they almost in unison rolled their shoulders forward like a garage door descending toward the pavement as it closed.

"I do have a bit of a question for both of you—when your son makes the necessary subtle changes to make school and life easier, what will you do? You reported this has been going on for 'years,' so I'm guessing that once he navigates these changes successfully, you'll have to think deeply about your relationship with him," I said.

If the parents symbolized defeat, their son represented a Marvel superhero breaking free from constraints, chest full of oxygen with arms raised to the sky. He was silently exploding with confidence. I realized then that we had already veered off the script onto a blank sheet of paper he could write on. I challenged the parents to think deeply about the change in their family unit simply by altering one variable: a troubled son transitioning into a healthy, normal teen. They operated as a family, bound by the narrative that he was bad and, therefore, negatively influenced the family. If that dynamic shifts, where will their bushel of complaints spill?

I learned a lot from working with that family. My intuition was correct, and the young man was a mix of brashness, boldness, kindness, creativity, and, best of all, he was interesting!

Unintentionally, Mom and Dad had acted as scene stealers, rarely allowing their son the chance to change the narrative. Words were weaponized on both sides to express frustration, assigning blame with each seemingly random outburst.

Dialogue didn't exist, and the power structure was built on the premise of "us" versus "them," underscoring the innate power parents are given to start the storylines of their children's lives. The young man's responsibility was to grasp that while he might not be able to alter the beginning, he sure had the opportunity to fill in the middle and present a future path he had an active hand in.

★ ★ ★

"The best weapon is to sit down and talk."

—*Nelson Mandela*

The story of Jonas in the previous chapter and the explosion of truth he displayed before the *judge, jury, and cadre* of European investors planted a seminal flag for me in the experiences that punctuate my addiction to discovering new angles on old, over-sold, and weathered stories. In fact, sometimes, it is those things that sit directly in front of us that we fail to see.

When I travel, I turn on the old-fashioned sensitivity radar to a decibel level meant, I think, for dogs, not humans. I wrench scene after scene, looking for something different. Architecture, music, food and the smell of food, nightlife, the impact of weather—you name it—I'm on the lookout for *it*.

After the applause from my live interview with Jonas faded, I reflected on the experience and the audience's reactions. The stage we shared resembled a TED Talk stage in its layout and relationship to the audience. Although it wasn't a TED Talk, our dialogue highlighted the importance of accepting circumstances and the role one takes to get the proverbial pen back on the page.

As I walked through the streets of Oslo, I found myself blending memories of my TEDx experience with the keynote address that Jonas and I had shared amidst a whirlwind of random interviews and social events centered around a week of sustainability stories. I had been advised to visit the Nobel Center—yes, the one that awards the Nobel Peace Prize! My official purpose in Norway was to capture Jonas's story along with those of other thought leaders. But what story would I seek by visiting the Nobel Center?

In retrospect, it was quite a silly question, which I attribute to sheer exhaustion and a desperate need to turn off my heat-seeking missile of a radar. Thankfully, a representative from the center accommodated my off-schedule detour. I had just finished back-to-back events, and I needed some time to just be. A quick change of direction, and I was minutes away from visiting the famous structure that housed some of the most influential representatives of various species.

On the water, the winds wrapped around and whipped over the Nobel Center and docked vessels with great confidence. I shook off the breeze as I walked in. The representative flashed a smile as if to say, "I know who you are, or you look like a tourist."

I was in the right spot.

She was a very pleasant woman who asked me if this was my first time at the Nobel Center and then inquired about my thoughts on the bench in front. "What bench?" I replied.

"The Best Weapon bench," she responded.

I quickly learned about the bench, "The Best Weapon," and immediately questioned why I had inadvertently turned off my *radar* earlier that day. I had missed something so simple yet utterly profound, and I had walked by it like I was strolling past park patrons. The bench was a piece of artwork named after the famous Nelson Mandela quote (provided earlier), symbolizing the need and power of dialogue.

My rendition of the bench to symbolize the grace and beauty of simplicity.

The bench symbolizes what is possible when two opposing views (people) sit on either side; its natural shape encourages dialogue between them. The symbolism is profound. The response to the bench and the initial campaign around dialogue quickly became a local fixture. Dialogue is now the guiding principle of the Nobel Center moving forward. This storyteller could not agree more with the center's decision—if they are curious about my opinion.

Again, I found myself staring at the *middle* of the bench, just like when I was contemplating the meat of my TEDx Talk or how I might provide an alternative to my therapeutic family's narrative. There appeared to me a Grand Canyon–sized lesson about the relative awareness that stories represent two entities and that any forward movement, together, would require dialogue.

The concept of the bench as a unifying object translates to the power of the foot-of-the-bed bench, where moms and dads tackle difficult conversations with their children, or park benches, where strangers can meet and greet one another while resting their outside arm on the shoulder of a city park bench. If the advent of the wheel advanced societies, then the invention of the bench platformed a story for generations to learn from and live by.

★ ★ ★

The dialogue bench disappears and reappears in different forms daily, giving all of us a chance to consider how our interactions at home and at work might play out. Waiting rooms, bus stops, conference rooms, athletic fields, therapeutic offices, and places of worship utilize benches to coach, direct, teach, proctor, and inform.

Most of us are confronted with the risks and rewards of engaging in these environments when we are the presumptive leading voice or the audience. Myopic agendas push away any chance of dialogue, while unfettered and disorganized words threaten accomplishment. This book doesn't intend to ride the torturous rails of geopolitics, but it would be narrative malpractice not to acknowledge the current world and the desperate need for dialogue.

Dialogue is a form of storytelling used when two parties seek an alternate ending to current, likely fractured circumstances and opposing storylines.

If you picked up this book in the 1960s, we would be discussing the need for dialogue in the United States to advance the Civil Rights Movement. In the 1980s, maybe we would be directed toward the AIDS epidemic and a clarion call to understand one another.

Personal stories of reflection often accompany discussions between two opposing parties. The power struggle of who outranks whom is dismantled during active dialogue, creating space for each entity's individual value to be acknowledged on equal footing. Scene stealers, as I previously noted, attempt to gain an upper hand by casually dismissing dialogue as a form of weakness.

Dialogue provides an opportunity for:

- Leaders to work through scenarios and strategic planning that includes multiple viewpoints.
- Entrepreneurs to explain their why to investors.
- Parents to explain complex issues with their children, including:
  - Death
  - The birds and the bees
  - Divorce
  - Moving
  - The loss of friends and the gain of new ones.

The benches may differ, but the consistent throughline to alignment remains unchanged. However, the packaging of this storytelling form is crucial for overcoming past gridlock.

★ ★ ★

My wife and I agreed that when each child reached the age of five, we would take them to Disney World—the golden age, she said, for a child to experience the magic of the Magic Kingdom. We had seen countless videos online of parents surprising their children with Christmas or birthday gifts, capturing the moment of bliss followed by hooting and hollering.

We had been saving money for our first Disney trip for some time, and we selfishly wanted to experience the same levels of joy as our internet *friends* had. We aimed to make it special for both them and us.

A scavenger hunt! That's it! We'll follow the kids around the house as they discover one clue after another until they finally open a box filled with Disney balloons eager to be released into the sky. I harkened back to my youth, at about the same age, when my family had the chance to go to Hawaii for the first time. There wasn't a scavenger hunt that day, but I vividly remember my younger sister crying because she didn't want to go to Hawaii (she was too young to understand), yelling that she wanted to go to Northern Michigan, to a place she knew.

I knew that I wanted to avoid a repeat performance with a new cast of characters—my children—to ensure a positive memory for all of us. I'd like to create a Norman Rockwell painting of complete family bliss, but I'd be stretching the truth over troubled waters. The kids marched around the house, finding clue after clue after clue (which is probably a hint in hindsight) so that by the time we reached the backyard and *the* box, our attitudes were deflated. The balloons emerged, and the kids looked up at us as if to say, "… what's all of this for?"

I was so influenced by the sights and sounds of countless perfectly timed Facebook family surprises that I forgot to consider my audience, including their age and attention levels, as well as the timing of the big reveal. I could have skipped a few steps and clues and headed straight for the ballot box.

★ ★ ★

Putting my lack of awareness of Mandela's bench aside, I worked hard to slide away from my embarrassment as we began to tour the Nobel Center. There were so many names and faces, and the room showcasing past Nobel Peace Prize winners is truly something to behold, surpassing the talents of your scribe— trust me, it's worth seeing if you ever have the chance. Glass canvases displaying recipient faces and pin lights guiding one through the intentionally dark and reflective space make one feel like they are floating among the greatest minds of our time.

We meandered through the exhibits, stopped for a brief conversation with the executive director of the center, and made our way down to the current exhibit.

The Echo Chamber, by famous Swedish artist Erik Johansson, provides an immersive experience that challenges visitors to explore their perceptions of the world. It challenges each visitor to look beyond their own echo chambers and what he calls filter bubbles. Broken into three photographic sections: The Echo Chamber, Filter Bubbles, and Painting a World of Our Own, Johansson encourages visitors to think not just about the impact societal schemas have on our sense of self but also about the roles we may unwittingly play in influencing the stories of others.

"Daring to take a step into the unknown and leave your comfort zone is something that has been recurring in my work for many years."

—*Erik Johansson*

As I gathered my belongings and stepped outside, I expressed gratitude to my guide, feeling as though I was saying only a temporary goodbye. I took in the simplicity of the bench dedicated to Nelson Mandela. That night, before closing up, I reached out to my Nobel guide to see if I could be connected to Johansson.

The trip ended, and I was headed back to the United States, if you will. I cobbled together a loosely coherent email to Johansson, hoping he'd humor me into a Zoom conversation about his work. I was already working on this book and thought that there must be something hidden in a prospective call with the artist.

Johansson responded almost immediately! We jumped on a Zoom call, on Halloween of all days, to discuss the nuances of interpretation in his work, his life in Prague, the capital of the Czech Republic, and his upcoming exhibits.

One exchange, in particular, stood out to me. I, too, question the pivotal role comfort plays in the stories we accept, those we resist, and those we wish we had the courage to join.

Rod: *Do you believe that your art brings you closer to humanity, or does it push you further away because of the questions it ultimately asks about them and society?*

Erik: *For many years, I've felt that I'm kind of standing a little bit on the edge—I'm next to society and looking into society and attempting to capture things that I find interesting about the society that I'm delving into.*

*Sometimes I feel like I'm not really participating [in society],
but then I feel like I am in other ways. I think a lot about the
elements of society that maybe people don't always talk about
or want to think about, but it still resonates with them when
they see it [his artwork].*

*I keep coming back to the concepts of echo chambers and
comfort zones. These concepts are quite personal, and for that
reason, I keep circling back to them. We naturally create
comfort zones for ourselves.*

*And for me, I guess it's fair to say that making images about
comfort zones has become my own form of a comfort
zone … which I'm trying to break free of.*

★ ★ ★

The notion of "coming together" rings loudly for me. From the
representative power of the dialogue bench in Oslo, Norway, to
its utility, the benches are different in form but aligned in their
opportunity for all of us to build awareness of others through
shared stories—called dialogue.

My TEDx Talk only came together when I set aside my
pride and perspective and reflected on the dialogues I had participated in over the years—those that cauterized emotional
experiences and created memorable moments to ponder over
time. I was inspired by the stories of others, and they, in large
part, co-authored the Talk I had longed to give for years.

The talk I likely would have given during the first go-round
would have missed the mark by focusing on my need to prove
myself to an audience echoing my perspective. It was only when I
engaged in dialogue across multiple continents, covering difficult
topics and histories, that I fully appreciated Gerver's words from a
decade earlier when he said my story hadn't been written yet.

★ ★ ★

To generate productive stories leveraging the power of dialogue, it is important to consider the following:

- Our willingness to be vulnerable in the stories we share cultivates connection through dialogue.
- The lack of dialogue leads one to jump to conclusions.
- Inherent power structures (for example, family therapy) and the implications of conversing *with* those in whom we are invested regarding the power our position conveys toward them.
- Effective negotiations of all kinds begin with productive dialogue.
- Effective dialogue addresses both sides of the issue to inform the origin of the problem and to project a shared vision.

How might your story differ if you dove into the middle instead of the beginning or the end?
How have predetermined endings limited your growth or opportunities?

I only shared the opening and concluding prose of my TEDx Talk to illustrate that before we speak truth to alternative endings, we must find peace with the beginning and gain an understanding of the middle to author the future we dream of.

Locate a bench. Fill in the blank spaces. Explore an alternate ending!

Sale! Worn bench. Needs elbow grease.

6

Selling Stories

The Power of Authenticity

Today I sell. Tomorrow I tell.

"The most powerful person in the world is the storyteller.
The storyteller sets the vision, values, and agenda of an entire
generation that is to come."

—Steve Jobs, co-founder of Apple

There was a time when I suited up five days a week and played the corporate game. The gig was at a technology company on the rise and relied on a single state contract to keep the lights on. It was a mix of startup veterans, recused corporate refugees, and consultants seeking semi-permanence. I can look back on the experience with fondness because of the opportunities I had to shape the author before you.

I believe I was designated as a vice president in title, but largely, I was an idea guy who was peering out over the dawn of podcasting and wondering, "What if?"

What if podcasting interviews with sector-specific leaders yielded strategic information? What would come of the subsequent relationships with guests I'd later hob-knob with at market events? Would we be seen in a favorable light? Could I impact the trajectory of the company?

I proposed a podcast to the executive team as part of my strategic communication plan. It wasn't that far from what I had already been doing: investor and bank presentations, conference representation, and brand building. The light was green, and I was off to configure my first podcast.

After outlining the necessary details (show name, cover art, social media, etc.), I set out to create a list of targeted voices I was eager to connect with, who likely held key market insights. I quickly compiled a list of guests who became former guests, and with each subsequent experience, I emailed another group of high achievers.

I was starting to recognize that people of all backgrounds enjoyed speaking about themselves in the form of stories about their work. The company I worked for was aiming to secure a state contract that would propel this startup to a scale up in no time.

My plan was to publicly interview officials connected to RFPs (requests for proposals) or tenders for my friends across the UK. These were state requests inviting vendors to apply—a murky world of, from what I could tell, side conversations, legacy partners, and wink-wink contract discussions. Now, this was the perspective of one individual, me, based loosely on a mix of pre-bid public meetings, previous interviews, and a Spidey-sense I've been honing since I was young. I systematically reached out to every possible layer of state office I believed was connected to or could be a future beneficiary of the executed contracted services.

The podcast interviews uncovered pain points, department-specific terminology, and key phrases, ultimately providing insight into the reality of the work they were pursuing. These seemingly minor points of value actually overshadow the information found in government tenders, which often leave applicants feeling uncertain.

My group didn't have to guess. We got it directly from the authors of the contract. Our response showcased our value proposition through the lens of the various pain points and phrases used by state leaders. We completed the final grouping—a success in its own right—and had to plan our presentation.

Little did I know that my journey was just beginning. Leadership assigned me the task of creating what would become our presentation, and they wanted me to deliver it. This was an incredible professional opportunity to explore my developing theories on the importance of reflecting on and reiterating the stories and language used by the very people determining our contractual fate.

A lot was expected of me, and I could feel the weight of every employee's contribution. There was a sense of pride in standing shoulder-to-shoulder with industry heavyweights. In the elevator at the state offices, I signed in quickly and took a moment to look into the eyes of those scheduled to present before us while faintly listening to those already sharing their vision. When it was our turn, we walked into what was likely an intentionally small room. The whole setup reminded me of countless movie scenes where a parole board sits side by side, each member holding a pen while papers neatly serve as a backdrop for clasped hands and curt smiles.

The only conceivable difference was that we were so close to the state officials that we could understand whispers passed along like a game of soup-can telephone. At one point during my presentation, the state director leaned over and said something akin to "… it's like they know our language." At that moment, with beads of sweat dangling from my hairline, it felt like a cool breeze brushing over my forehead. Why wouldn't they want to work with a company that spoke their language? I was certain we would win!

We certainly did!

That started a multiyear collaboration that firmly placed the startup in the scale-up category. I was flying high! I had successfully leveraged storytelling within a business setting, creating value across the company. Months later, I was called into a C-suite meeting—a random early-week meeting in the CEO's office that became one of the more pivotal moments in my understanding of my own value.

I'd like to think that one C-suite member has found a replacement for this rather thin bravado. However, at that time, his leadership style combined elements of a frat guy with shots from the 1987 Oliver Stone film *Wall Street*, featuring the character Gordon Gekko played by Michael Douglas.

This guy thrived on fear and seemed to enjoy it. Several topics were discussed, including sales and sales tactics that were either effective or needed to be retired. For some reason, Mr. Gekko turned to me and said abruptly, "It's not like you've ever sold anything!" I was in complete shock, so much so that I, unprofessionally, snapped back with little regard for my job. Cooler heads prevailed, but the message was imprinted on my psyche, creating deep anxiety about whether I would constantly have to prove my worth.

I can look back and appreciate the value of the experience. I know the company experiences similar appreciation each time that contract is renewed year after year. Everybody won, and I learned a valuable lesson.

Selling a vision also involves promoting ourselves and the value we bring to the organizations we represent.

I successfully packaged a story and vision for the work itself, but I neglected to embed my own narrative to ensure my contributions reflected the value of my presence. I left my fate in the hands of insecure leaders who perceived my input as threatening. Only later did I realize the power of storytelling in business, but I always opined …

What if Steve Jobs had been in that meeting …?

★ ★ ★

The Scene: A suburban elementary school gym.

The characters include seven nine-year-old boys: some lanky, some stocky; some knowledgeable about playing, while others are participating in the sport for the very first time. There's an immigrant, a child on the autism spectrum, a couple of wise guys, including the coach (me), and several vocal parents who are hoping for a *successful* season of youth basketball.

I signed up to coach my then nine-year-old son's basketball team, fully aware that the likelihood of striking talent gold was fleeting. I attended the draft (in my day, they just assigned kids to rosters coached by dads) and was taken aback by the competitive nature of the other fathers—we even had trades! I may not be the brightest bulb, but I quickly realized that the supposed talent was being scooped up fast, leaving me to assume that the final rounds were made up of kids who would be considered bench warmers.

Aside from having an inner dialogue about how wrong it all felt, I knew I needed to leave that gym with a roster of players. If I sensed a kid was being left off one roster, I snatched them up and added them to mine. If we were going to be a squad of *Bad News Bears* (1976 classic film), then I'd play the character of Walter Matthau, minus his tendency for alcohol.

Practices came and went, but I remained focused on one thing—helping these boys feel like they were truly part of a team. I didn't worry about points scored or wins and losses, even as the "Ls" piled up. We were having fun, developed a practice routine, and slowly but surely demonstrated progress in the only ways *cubs* can.

As the season came to a close, we faced an unstoppable team. Reflecting on the experience of the draft, it was evident that this team had played together for several seasons.

I *really* wanted to beat them …

It didn't start well. Layup after layup, the other team had me questioning their ages. We looked around as if we weren't entirely sure what should come next. I stayed true to myself as I wrestled with what to do. I had to make a change! Halftime was approaching, and we were down 18–2. Seconds ticked away, and I decided to call a timeout—a clear violation of the unwritten rule to let the inevitable proceed swiftly in youth sports. The referees looked at me like, "Hey coach, there's less than a minute left until halftime."

I hurried all my players into a makeshift circle. I looked at my son, who I'd like to think takes after me, a bulldog who never fears the height, weight, or skill level of his opponent, and said, "One stop!" He nodded in agreement. I pointed to the scoreboard, acknowledging that things didn't look good for us. I continued, "Boys, it's their ball. They will NOT score before halftime! We will, at all costs, win this possession and then come back here at halftime to devise a plan to mount a comeback!" The piercing horn of the clock operator rang out, and I held my son back in a way only a dad can.

"When they cross half court, I want you to take both hands and smack the floor. Got it?" No verbal response was necessary. He understood that the message he was sending was just as much for our players as it was a signal to our opponent that this wasn't over.

The whistle blew, the ball was handed over at the baseline, and they started to dribble toward our basket. My son looked at me, and I nodded. The point guard crossed halfcourt, and my son smacked the floor like he was punching through an eternity of hate. The point guard was rattled, and as the seconds ticked down, we caused a turnover, and the horn sounded.

This was a small but significant victory for our squad. Since halftime always felt like a pitstop at a Formula 1 race, I had little time to organize the plan I promised just moments ago I'd have for our comeback.

"Grab water, boys." I look at the clock spiraling toward zero.

"Okay, come here. Boys, come on!"

"Here's what I know, boys. They think they have this in the bag, and they expect us to just fall over.

That's not going to happen today! Look at the score! Look at it! Now, we may not score enough points to come back and win—so what we're going to do is make this the toughest game they've ever played. I don't care if we fail to score even one more point—they will not score another basket today! OKAY? Okay? Our focus will be on stealing the ball, rebounding, and boxing out—that's it!"

I scanned the boys' eyes. They were glued to me. This wasn't typical coach talk. I wasn't just a dad coaching his son's team. No, I was shaking up their little competitive spirits ... and I knew it. I had one last plea as the clock ticked from 30 to 29 seconds before the start of the second half.

"Boys, I know this is a mighty mountain to climb. But we're going to do it! Who wants to climb a mountain with me today?"

I have no clue what this diatribe looked like from the stands, and I can only squeamishly think some of the parents were developing a diagnosis for their coach. Thankfully, and quite immediately, the boys, like falling dominoes or kids jumping on desks, proclaim Robin Williams, in *Dead Poets Society* (1989), as their captain, sequentially shouting, "Captain, my Captain!"

"I'll climb with you coach!"

"Count me in!"

"Yes!"

The final confirmatory response went to the one player who was likely to check a box stating that he tried basketball, not that he played basketball. A sweet kid who, with great comedic timing, casually said, "Eh, I don't feel like climbing a mountain today, Coach Rod."

A hearty laugh rippled through the entire team, providing a moment of levity amidst the backdrop of great mythical wars.

Final score: Bad News Bears 22, Seasoned Vets 20

When the final horn rang out, the boys and I felt as if we had either survived an epic tornado or summitted the highest peak—either way, we were winners!

We huddled together in the corner of the gym as the next set of teams started warming up. Our parents began to arrive, creating a sound barrier against the bouncing balls and scoreboard horns.

"Boys, I am so proud of you! We decided as a group to change the way our opponents experienced us, and we held them to two points in the second half! Two!! Soak up this moment!!

We will all remember this story for years to come. From now on, we will be the best defensive team in this league!"

I loved that team!

We had a successful playoff run, though our season ultimately came to an end. I learned a great deal about myself and the power of storytelling to convey a vision while understanding my audience of nine-year-olds and connecting with them on the emotional rollercoaster of youth sports.

★ ★ ★

There isn't a prerequisite for being a good storyteller; you don't have to channel an iconic coach to explore the boundaries of your voice or the acceptability of your tone. I sold a vision and utilized the personality traits of the boys I had come to know for the collective good. Even though a leader, in name only, in a corporate environment told me I couldn't sell anything, I had the receipts with the endorsements of seven young men who tested their limits and learned something about themselves on a cold February morning in suburbia.

Considerations

- Team stories, whether on the hardwood or in the office, present an opportunity for others to feel a sense of belonging to purpose, strategy, or community.
- Creating stories that include the audience's world fosters buy-in across games, projects, challenges, and opportunities.
- Telling stories either widens the gap between you and your audience or raises doubts about your ability to understand their current perspective or position.

If I hadn't put the time in to run and sweat with the boys during practices or pregame layup lines, my William Wallace call to defend the court would have died before it left my lips. We don't have to be Mel Gibson (*Braveheart*, 1995) and full-throated to influence those around us. Remember, storytelling is a lot like listening to or creating a great song—there is a rhythm to reading an audience that can only be learned through consistent curiosity about the world around us and the stories that help us comprehend the grandeur of it all.

★ ★ ★

Around the time I was labeled as someone who couldn't sell, I stumbled upon an opportunity to work with Vanderbilt University's business school (Owen Graduate School of Management), a relationship that ended up lasting nearly two decades. Most of my work focused on graduate students pursuing their Master of Accountancy (MAcc) degree from what many refer to as the "Harvard of the South." Each year, I was invited during orientation week to work with fresh-faced students, still on the edge of adulthood, who had made significant career and financial choices to attend Vanderbilt.

As spring turned the corner into the sweltering months of summer across middle Tennessee, I reached out to department leaders and requested the resumes of the 40–50 students I would soon meet in early August. It became clear early on that if I wanted to find an edge to apply to my work, I needed to do my homework. I would download and print the resumes, then sit down with a pen and a yellow highlighter, looking for unique data points attributed to each student.

I would look for home of origin, unique naming conventions (double first names in the South), unique undergraduate experiences, or study abroad programs—anything that would help me learn about the team I was about to "coach" for a few days under the unforgiving August southern sun. At first, I thought it would be relatively easy to find unique attributes in each student.

It wasn't; in fact, it was almost impossible.

Practically every resume looked the same except for the undergraduate programs. They all boasted relatively high grade point averages (GPAs), secured similar internships, and showcased common accomplishments as if they had just negotiated the purchase of Alaska on March 30, 1867, for $7.2 million from Russia. These inflated achievements, across the board, indicated to me that I needed to dig deeper, so I decided to reluctantly scour social media accounts.

I needed to discover what was interesting about these students.

Thankfully, students remained largely unaware (not meant in a derogatory way) of those who pay attention to the posts they make across various platforms. A real treasure trove of information started to emerge.

Over the years, and perhaps through the graduating class's transfer of knowledge to new students, I started to discover more stories without the same depth of exploration that I had in the early years. Our sessions always began with a round-robin conversation, everyone sitting in a circle discussing the narratives their resumes conveyed. Gradually, students caught on—I was looking for the stories beneath and just around the corner from their resumes. I shared with them that they were effectively "burying the lead" on the narratives that had defined them up until now.

They weren't selling themselves. They were presenting themselves as static, immobile products to be gazed at or gawked at. The only authentic aspect of the story they were portraying was the headshot photo attached to the resume.

To drive the point home, we discussed the concept of *Positional Power*—the notion that if I take away your business card and title or rank, how will you communicate the value you provide in the context of your work? Authority derived from one's position tells a story through email signatures, business cards, and online profiles.

We focused not on what they had done, but rather on who they are, through a series of sequential activities aimed at challenging convention (for example, I chose this degree program because I have family members who are accountants) and encouraging deeper contemplation of the stories that generate interest. The MAcc students quickly understood the importance of discovering their own narratives—Vanderbilt, in partnership with the Big 4 Accounting firms, organized regular social events for the students to connect with the firms they would soon apply to.

To prepare the students, we started with some basic and natural separators: What was their motivation for entering the program, and what was their greatest fear about selecting this profession?

The cohort quickly coalesced around shared concerns regarding technology integration and the potential of artificial intelligence (AI) on job security, leading them to question whether they would remain committed to the profession and industry in the long run. The team dynamic was solidifying, and the veneer of expected stories and responses, like clockwork, began to fade away. The middle innings of the program proved to be a gauntlet for the students as I handed the baton of speaking over to them.

Creating two circles, one facing outward and serving as the center of a bicycle wheel, I had the students remain seated for the entire exercise. The other students stood at the end of the "spokes," facing inward toward the center of the bicycle. I rotated questions among the group and had them take turns asking and answering the same questions. Then, I yelled "stop" over the crescendo of talkative twenty-somethings and instructed the outer circle to rotate one seat to the left.

Why?

Each time a session began (lasting no more than five minutes), the students had the opportunity to answer questions that encouraged them to share their own stories, not the ones they felt compelled to present, but tales that would likely foster connections among their peers.

The inner circle felt confined, while the students actively rotating around the center felt refreshed, even though both groups had to ask and answer the same questions. Each time a story was shared, confidence visibly grew. Most students leaned into their stories and extended the same courtesy in listening to their colleague's story.

They not only learned about the parts of their story that evoked positive reactions, but also about their classmates, who provided rich narratives that showcased their strengths to prospective recruiters and highlighted their classmates' unique value propositions.

A sample of the questions is as follows:

- What did you want to be as a child?
- What makes you unique?
- How do you believe others perceive you?
- How do you justify your value to the firm?

The questions gradually became more challenging, enhancing each student's narrative skills and giving them an advantage in sharing their stories, emotions, and the duration they could engage purposefully. They stopped worrying about finding the right answer for the right story and began exploring narratives buried in their minds that they had either forgotten or discarded due to a perceived lack of market value.

If you assume that your audience shares foundational similarities with you, push yourself to explore other storylines that have aided you along your professional path. You never know who will respond or what future collaborations might develop.

To conclude each session, I displayed several 8 × 11 pictures, similar to story prompts, for them to choose from based on the day's overarching question. This created an opportunity for each of them to turn their prior experiences into a means of self-promotion through storytelling. The question most frequently used was poignant yet broad enough for students to weave together a narrative with a beginning, middle, and end without my needing to instruct them explicitly. What is the greatest misconception about you?

The majority of students began with what we could see:

- Most people think I'm aloof because I'm shy.
- Most people think I'm not serious because I like to have a good time.
- Most people assume I don't have an opinion because I'm quiet.

The list continued until they linked the external perceptions to past accomplishments and scenarios, culminating in an inevitable request from classmates for accountability throughout the process—accountability to their goals, not their character.

The lessons may have taken a few decades to solidify in my mind, but the work I did with MAcc students strengthened my understanding that to promote myself, my vision, or the products I eventually developed, I needed to lean forward. If I could authentically convey this, the spirit of my "ask" would be received with the intent forged through years of effort.

★ ★ ★

For each of us, there is a natural evolution of story that offers cover, opportunity, clarity, and windows to peer through, revealing the dreams we have built over a lifetime. The enhanced opportunity to quote and sell ourselves aids in constructing unique, compelling narratives that inspire both others and ourselves throughout our lives.

Often, a delicate balance between humility and hubris leads us to edit storylines while maintaining an eye for authenticity. I wish I could say, based on my experience, that once we define the boundary lines, we can simply check a box and move on. You'll discover, as I have, that there are moments in our lives that require different stories and storytelling methods to make a point, advocate for the marginalized, explore opportunities, and embrace fleeting moments that can propel you beyond the dreams you've long gazed at through the window of your mind.

★ ★ ★

As luck would have it, I opened an email from a seasoned public relations professional pitching a story about two Pacific Northwest moms, Kelly Oriard and Callie Christensen, who left the fields of education and mental health to create educational characters that now have their own show on Apple TV+. I've always enjoyed a good, unexpected story, so I thought, "Why not?" and decided to take a chance on this dynamic duo.

They had been friends through school and continued that friendship as they navigated marriage, kids, divorce, and entrepreneurship. As we concluded the podcast interview that would later become an article in *Forbes*, they suggested I talk to the woman they had referenced in the interview as the spark to the flame that was now burning across television sets in the form of cute, cuddly stuffed animals rich with social-emotional skills.

The woman they mentioned was none other than the president of television at The Jim Henson Company.

Yeah, that Jim Henson, famous for the Muppets.

Part of the benefits package of my work, said with sappy sarcasm, is spending time with fantastic storytellers who regularly ignite creative fires that burn long after our interview. I was absolutely interested in being connected with Halle Stanford of Henson for a background interview on the creators of Slumberkins!

The interview was scheduled, and I launched Zoom as I had done countless times before. I felt tense. I wanted not only to present myself as a like-minded storytelling expert but also to learn as much as I could from Halle. Thankfully, the interview became a fun-filled adventure through a roller rink of stories—vivid, suspenseful, enlightening, and inspiring. I felt as if I had been given a last-minute chance to play jazz piano and made the most of my creative session with Halle.

As Halle's beaming smile—those who know her understand what I mean—faded through the pixels of Zoom, I ripped my headphones off my head and quickly called my wife.

"That went so well! She was incredible! I really think I should pitch her my TV show idea, but I probably only have today to do it—I'll be just like any other interviewer by tomorrow." I could hear my wife's finger tapping her temple as if to say, "… here he goes again …"

I'll own it.

One of the downsides of living in a perpetual story is that life can feel like a bit of a choose-your-own-adventure, even when it comes to big, consequential decisions. I hung up, emailed the publicists who had arranged the interview, and requested Halle's email address.

Crickets.

An anticipated non-response attributed to someone simply doing their job to protect the privacy of those they represent wouldn't deter me. Armed with a couple of email-finding apps, I was in business. I sent an email thanking Halle for a wonderful conversation and then took my shot: "If you're ever looking for a show idea that combines kids, globetrotting, and puppets, I'd love to share my idea with you!"

If it had been just a few years ago, I would have ended the email there, selling my story and accomplishments short. I had worked too hard and had already pitched show ideas to NBC Universal and National Geographic.

So, I thought, hmm ... how can I share my story visually in a way that suits the moment?

I knew it (fists pumped in the air, teeth clenched)! I created a one-sheet visual bio, fully aware that most email servers display a preview of attachments. I got to work, leafing through count-less photos of people, places, and events, understanding that a positive response to my query would only come if she felt my background warranted review.

I couldn't just provide a standard and woefully dull resume. I needed to capture the accomplishments and authenticity of my work just like I had conveyed to MAcc students for years.

It worked!

Later that day, Halle responded enthusiastically, punctuated by a cheerful array of happy-face emojis. Perhaps it was the photo of me with Pope Francis or the guest list she shared—at that moment, I didn't care. I had created an opportunity, and to be honest, I sold my first story!

The story of me!

We are still proudly in the throes of selling our television show, and I continue to learn with each pitch we make to studio executives. Each time we co-pitch with my co-creator and puppeteer extraordinaire, Victor Yerrid, I reflect on the initial pitch because without it, we wouldn't be here.

★ ★ ★

When we get it right, our stories sell our abilities and talents and generate opportunities to create new stories with other creators, companies, innovators, and teams. The summit is surely formidable, but the opportunity to author stories, including our dreams, with those who inspire us underscores the potential to sell others on the merits we've achieved.

I may never sell a piece of technology, but I'll definitely sell the heck out of a halftime story, and those who have me ping-ponging around the planet with a puppet in the name of storytelling.

"After nourishment, shelter and companionship, stories are what we need most in the world."

Sir Phillip Pullman

Sir Phillip Pullman, regarded by *The Times* as one of the 50 greatest British writers since 1945, aptly describes the transom my MAcc students had to cross to understand that their stories are not merely nice-to-haves but essential to attaining the futures they dream of.

Looking for authenticity. Settle for truth.

7 | Reflection

The Power of Version Control

'I' in team. You in perpetuity.

"I am not a role model! Just because I dunk a basketball doesn't mean I should raise your kids."
—Charles Barkley (Nike, 1993)

Perspective.

Having it suggests a certain level of awareness.

To lose perspective ...

Perspective as a storyteller means having a firm grasp of the story from multiple angles. In life and in relation to others, perspective has the opportunity to gift grace to each party. Telling good stories is as much about perspective as it is about timing and situational awareness. The delivery mechanism is underscored by reflection—the act of cobbling together a series of moments into a shared tale, providing the run-of-show

117

elements and tied off with lessons learned destined to impact future moments.

Version control plays a crucial role in the overall narrative that unfolds on stage, during a cellphone exchange, or in front of a judge or jury. As storytellers, we possess the final say in determining which sequences make it and which end up on the proverbial cutting room floor.

Deconstructing these basic tenets allows us to reflect on the story told.

In short, our retelling of the same story will reflect the impact the story had on us as an audience.

In the early 1990s, Nike was struggling to find its footing, no pun intended, through the stories of athletes who were not Michael Jordan for American male teenagers. Charles Barkley, a known irritant and tell-it-like-you-see-it Dream Teamer, wasn't exactly the grand marshal of a Nike "Be like Mike" ad campaign.

Globally recognized, yes.

Accomplished, yes.

Intriguing, absolutely!

Somewhere between corporate lore and reality, the ad campaign "I'm not a role model" emerged, featuring Sir Charles. It became an instant talking point for sports reporters, national news outlets, and newspapers, with everyone asking who kids should look up to. The highly successful ad agency Wieden+Kennedy responded to the calls from Nike executives to create an ad campaign aimed at teenage males, and they, along with Barkley, delivered.

The spot had an air of independence.

It was storytelling without the preamble.

Only the sizzle.

The ad reflected the sentiment of the buyers that Nike was seeking. Storytelling at its finest.

It struck a representative nerve even in the locker rooms of Rochester High School in suburban Detroit, where I grew up. Barkley wasn't a member of my treasured Bad Boys (Detroit Pistons), but his outspoken and raw approach screamed teenage angst across the country.

An important footnote to the story lies in the crafted version and the real-life incident. The advertisement was inspired by an on-court event that occurred two years before the bold Nike ad. After tolerating a reported racist heckler in the stands, Barkley spat in the direction of the verbal assailant, only to miss and hit an eight-year-old girl. As a result, Barkley was fined $10,000 and suspended for one game due to the incident in New Jersey.

Luckily, I had the privilege of sharing the impact of that commercial with Charles when I interviewed him for an article I wrote a few years ago. Barkley, a father and now grandfather, reflected on the commercial and his current stance, sticking true to the essence of the 1993 ad—in part, *role models should be those you live with and who are in your community, not athletes.*

Telling the story of his story's impact back to him left me feeling incredibly vulnerable in the moment. Charles was as advertised and then some during our time together, reflecting on a hallowed career on and off the court. He even took a few minutes to speak with my rabid fan and son, creating an instant story from a singular moment in time.

★ ★ ★

I had recently been named editor at large of an international online publication called Fair Observer. This journalistic oddity is centered not on clickbait or assumed newsmakers but global narratives told through the eyes of retired diplomats and ambassadors, former intelligence officers from several NATO countries, and think tank leaders narrowly focused on extending prior posts into legacy plays—a real who's who of the geopolitical bingo card.

I was, dare I say, out of my element and once again found myself to be the least intelligent person in the room. It was a challenge I embraced wholeheartedly—a chance to capture stories from naturally stoic individuals, whether by personality or profession, whose primary responsibility was to maintain a death grip on national secrets. I was given absolute freedom to reach out to anyone who had either been written about or who had contributed to the pages of Fair Observer, which is read in more than 90 countries.

The list of potential interview guests for my new Fair Observer podcast was as deep as the ocean and as vast as a Texas early morning horizon line. The only solution I could think of was to select a series of guests over a discrete period of time— one to sharpen my skills through "forced" and repeated conversations and interviews, hoping to improve with each subsequent guest, and two to select people whom I was naturally curious to know.

The inaugural guest was a Vietnam veteran, David Holdridge, who had served as an infantry platoon leader outside of Chu Lai. After being critically wounded and needing more than 18 months to recover, Holdridge spent 40 years working with humanitarian organizations that served populations depleted in spirit and resources from war, exploitation, and impoverishment across West Africa, the Middle East, and Asia.

This was my guy! I was sure he had a wealth of knowledge and stories to share during our interview. David graciously accepted my invitation for an interview, and days later, I found myself peering through the pixelated wonder of Zoom into David's home office. He instantly reminded me of a neighbor I might have had in the past or a friendly gentleman who shared an afternoon with me, waiting for the oil change on our cars to finish. He offered nothing but himself and the stories that chronicled his time in Vietnam.

A fearless storyteller, never short on words, he had a gravelly voice that initially caught me off guard. The sound of him searching for air to breathe grounded my tone, setting a rhythm to the interview.

Question asked.

Breath taken.

Answer provided.

Inhale … words riding parallel to exhaled breath … again and again.

After my initial startle, I settled into the jazz session we appeared to share jointly. In the moment, my only thought was what it would be like to hear David, not as the dark villain of Darth Vader voiced by the late great James Earl Jones, but as a veteran taking a hill to share a piece of his story with all of us.

Quite quickly, I felt a sense of responsibility wash over me—I had one opportunity to capture this man's story with dignity, accuracy, and respect. This wasn't a time to be whimsical with the questions I volleyed over; it was a time to harness situational awareness as a storyteller. Here is an excerpt of a story David shared upon being critically injured:

David: *There was this nurse—when they took me off the medevac helicopter and pushed me into the Quonset hut, she bent*

*over close and soft and asked me my religion, and I was
able to spit out …*

… Am I going to die? (David's retelling voice
clenched with desperation, at the threshold of life
and death)

Nurse: *No, we have to ask that.*

David: *I looked up at her, and she was everything I didn't have
out in the field, her face was kind, and it was beautiful to
my eyes because it was nothing like what I was living out
there on the perimeter, on the outside and I said, "Kiss me.
Kiss me" and then the pentothal hit.*

David later revealed that the nurse he briefly loved was
Sharon Ann Lane (July 7, 1943–June 8, 1969). Sharon was a U.S.
Army nurse and the only American servicewoman killed as a
direct result of enemy fire during the Vietnam War.

That day, I made a friend.

I hope he did, too.

★ ★ ★

I think it's fair to say that most of us live relatively complicated
lives made up of a matrix of internal and external challenges at
home, work, and across our respective communities. David's
retelling of the toils of war serves as a reminder that the stories
we share and reflect on aren't just regurgitated moments inter-
spersed with laughter or tears or both. I am often reminded by
the Davids in my life that:

1. Sometimes, the initial story isn't the one that ultimately
   resonates. As narrators of a tale, we have a choice about
   the sequence, tone, tenor, and biases we weave into our
   prose.

2. Heightened awareness of the power of the pen or microphone should prompt active, internal questioning about the version (of the story) to be told and why.
3. Acknowledging that minor characters or plotlines may serve as the hairpin trigger for someone else's experience.

This isn't to say we shouldn't write and tell stories from our perspective. Quite the opposite—truly great storytelling and storytellers recognize the significant nature of characters in conflict, both seen and unseen. It is this awareness that creates perspectives with conviction. You don't have to be or like the villain, but it wouldn't hurt to consider the collateral impact on them through the tale you're about to weave.

The art of imagining ourselves in others' shoes has long served many a husband well when thinking pregame about how to discuss a sensitive and potentially explosive topic with his spouse. For the record, my wife is far better than your current guide, hence the value I put on one's ability to think methodically and thoughtfully before conveying a position through storytelling.

To clarify, the intentional choice to reflect on the stories we plan to share positions us much better than starting with tone-deaf messaging that quickly diminishes the energy of even the most entrepreneurial settings. I have personally utilized reflection in storytelling during keynote presentations, when contemplating a potentially delicate question I wish to pose to a guest, and when seeking to align missions and motivations in corporate contexts.

Considerations

The next time you have an opportunity to speak before your colleagues, leadership team, students, or family members, consider using stories that link two different points in time through your narrative.

- Share a story about a past experience and connect your memory to today's goal.
  - This will undoubtedly lead you to questions about the audience you will be speaking to, whether it is an audience of one during a job interview or a ballroom full of people at a conference.
  - You will consider their origins, professional backgrounds, potential subject matter, and current events that are near and dear to them.
- The overarching goal is to find a morsel of shared connection or opportunity that you can incorporate into your own telling of a story you'd ultimately like them to engage in.

★ ★ ★

As an alum of Michigan State University and a proud Spartan, the "Go Green, Go White" call unites current and former students and faculty around the world. Like most universities, there are official and unofficial ambassadors of the collegiate brand that transcend generations. Maybe not all, but most Spartans proudly bellow the name of alum Earvin "Magic" Johnson when asked about famous and universally respected representatives. To live in the state of Michigan almost requires a universal love for Magic, even if he played for the vaunted Los Angeles Lakers during the heyday of the Pistons.

It was with the weight of a state (hyperbole engaged) that I accepted an invitation to interview Magic in person in Los Angeles a few years back. After the initial excitement and the smattering of high-fives from my kids, it hit me!

I'm interviewing Magic! The Magic who ripped my heart out in 1988 and whom I painted for a fourth-grade art project. Look, I told myself, you've interviewed several "magical" people, and this Magic was just another addition to the list.

That lasted as long as it took to glide across the freeway of my inner dialogue.

I prepared for the interview, letting go of my natural instinct to be in the moment and react to the energy in the room. I was zeroed in on the first question I would pose to Magic. If I didn't get off on the right foot, I'd be in tangible trouble.

The hotel suite, retrofitted for the interview, had everything you might expect: people on walkie-talkies, assistants bringing in bottles of water, random voices from around corners calling for snacks, publicists, production staff, and me. I had been given a solid few weeks to decide how I wanted to conduct the interview, but I kept forgetting the basics. I was so anxious about appearing foolish that I didn't realize we were both Spartans.

Lighting check, sound check, water supply ... check. All we needed was for Magic to show up. That was definitely an understatement. Magic is a towering presence who changes the atmosphere of any room he enters. Perhaps out of nerves and not following best practices, one of the sound technicians approached Magic to get him mic'd up. Calling balls and strikes, I would say he was a bit too aggressive toward Magic, and the tension rippled through the room.

For me, Magic's "Hold on there!" might as well have pressed the reset button on my brain. The production staffer inadvertently soiled the mood. I knew Magic was miffed, as I would have been, and I'm not Magic Johnson.

At that exact moment, a reset was just what I needed. I returned to the fundamental basics and, instead of asking a question or engaging in what was expected, I said:

"Well, Magic, I guess we're just a couple of Spartans hanging out in L.A."

That magical smile and laugh leaped out, and instead of a handshake, the Magic Man embraced me.

(Blood pressure returning to normal in 3, 2, 1.)

To say I was exuberant inside would vastly underestimate the relief I felt and the connection I had instantly made with a global icon. As for the first question—I tossed it out of the metaphorical window and doubled down on my reflection to include his impact on me as a boy.

For context, it was June 1988, and my beloved Detroit Pistons were the team I would sneak away to watch late at night during West Coast road trip games. Unbeknownst to them, they dictated my emotional state many mornings after wins and losses as I walked the hallways of school. Game 7 was down to the wire, a tense back-and-forth the whole time. The ball was passed down to Hall of Famer Kareem Abdul-Jabbar, who went into his famous sky hook shot. He misses!!! We were seconds away from our first championship, but the whistle of injustice pierced the speaker on my television set. A foul was called on the original Bad Boy, Bill Laimbeer, whose reputation for backyard bully-ball precedes him.

Later known as the "Phantom Foul," Magic's Lakers—not my Pistons—raised the NBA championship trophy, and I was left sobbing at what might have been. Let's not forget that at the tender age of 11, time didn't move at the same speed it does now. No, the hands of time crept along like a sloth, making the wait of an entire offseason and then a season for retribution utterly devastating.

As the production team counted us down, "… in 5, 4, 3, 2, 1," and pointed at me, I looked at Magic and said…

"Let's be honest, Magic, to this Bad Boy, that *was* a phantom foul in 1988 that ripped my heart out, right?"

Side note—I knew I was pinging the risk meter, fearful that even my green and white blood wouldn't protect me from Magic's ire.

In only the way Magic can, he responded with a Santa-like guttural laugh, one I then joined in on, and we were off and running through a moment in time I'll never forget, as a Spartan and a dedicated storyteller.

★ ★ ★

As a youth, you might assume that my bedroom ceiling never had enough space for me to cross enemy lines with a Magic Johnson poster, and you'd be right. However, the intertwining and emotionally connected stories of the Detroit athletes and teams that adorned my ceiling with the likes of fellow Spartan Magic Johnson are now firmly ingrained in my approach.

I had almost accidentally stumbled upon a bit of storytelling pixie dust with Magic. Maybe the audio assistant's brash approach to mic'ing up Magic actually helped in my eventual delivery, or maybe it was as simple as two Spartans hanging out in L.A. Either way, meeting the moment sometimes requires that we dig into our own vault of experiences to find a connection with others on which to reflect. Sharing that journey with them can thrust interactions rich with reflection, shared emotion, and unique experiences for audiences.

Cautionary Moments

Stories rooted in reflection ("When I reflect …") are inherently subjective, shaped by the concluding emotions and feelings of the storyteller. The speaker—whether a CEO, HR hiring manager, little league coach, or other—holds complete control of the narrative, which can lead to a bias that shades in the lines of the story. This doesn't imply that people approach acts of reflection with malice, but rather that the influence of the moment can tempt embellishment, a revisionist historical interpretation, or, in a darker sense, even propaganda.

I like to think about the following points when I consider reflection as a tool to connect or engage through storytelling. Assume that the term *audience* refers interchangeably to a spectrum of one to many.

- Do I have enough data points to suggest that the audience's response will be positive?
- Will reflecting on their public story create a forced response that separates me from the goal of connecting with them?
- If my rationale for reflecting on their public story is merely entertainment or to secure a joke, I should double down on my research to ensure that good-hearted humor is a part of the culture.

One could argue that I took a risk by reflecting on Magic and the Lakers' public moment of beating my Pistons for the NBA championship. On the surface, that might seem true, but Magic had, moments before, embraced me as part of his community with a hug and conversation about East Lansing and MSU. I doubled down to lay the groundwork for questions I ultimately wanted to explore that, overall, were thought-provoking for the audience to experience.

Without the shared connection of the Spartan community, I would most likely have found another route to meet my objective—to be interesting and provide Magic with a fresh interview experience. In fact, the question I am most proud of during that exchange had nothing to do with basketball or reflecting on the tears of an 11-year-old—the question that triggered Magic to say, "You know, I've never been asked that before ..." was about mental health for entrepreneurs.

Embrace vulnerability through reflective stories that highlight your intentions and foster trust across audiences of all shapes and sizes.

★ ★ ★

We had just celebrated the transition from one year to the next, and like many, the new year was a chance for me to be optimistic about the unknown that would surely reveal exciting developments. I received a message on social media from a leader at Michigan State University. She wanted to gauge my interest in giving the keynote speech at the annual MSU Alumni Summit later that spring. The answer was an easy yes, but the responsibility ahead quickly oriented me to the meaning of the event.

This event was scheduled to take place on campus, in the same building that, only a year prior, had been the site of a horrific shooting that claimed the lives of three students and injured several more. It would be the first formal gathering held in the building, and this leader believed a keynote address about storytelling would be fitting. Through managing group therapy sessions, I captured the stories of children who were victims of abuse. I worked one-on-one with individuals who had witnessed great trauma and helped people whose daily goal was to manage their self-harm tendencies. I had never before been invited to participate in an event at the very location where lives had been lost.

I knew I wanted to find a thread, a collection of stories to reflect on that had substance and hopefully meaning for the audience. I was informed that one of the speakers joining me on stage would be T.J. Duckett, an MSU and NFL alum who was selected in the first round (18th overall) of the 2002 NFL Draft by the Atlanta Falcons. On one hand, the sports fan in me was excited to meet T.J., but on the other hand, I was perplexed about the pairing. Were we giving individual speeches or some combination? I wasn't sure. I did some quick research to find out what happened for T.J. after his very productive professional football career, and I was struck by his commitment to his community and others. He wasn't the bruising running back I remembered from television. He was speaking, volunteering, and appeared to be a deeply spiritual man.

I figured it out! I suggested that instead of having two somewhat adjacent speaking spots, why not bring T.J. on stage after my keynote for a moderated discussion? Think of it like a fireside chat, but updated with questions that draw out T.J.'s core message through storytelling and my curiosity. Everyone liked the idea, and T.J. and I hopped on a quick call to sync up. I was thoughtful, engaging, and very likable.

The day arrived, and wearing a new suit—green, of course—I entered the building on a glorious Midwest spring day. A lovely introduction set the stage for me to discuss the power of storytelling through several of my adventures. Naturally, I would have been a fool not to share the image of Magic and me laughing about the "phantom" foul captured by a production assistant that day. I transitioned from lessons learned to audio clips of interviews that, in my estimation, carried the weight of the moment. I recounted tales from my journeys across Africa and reflected on the significance of the ordinary in showcasing the strength of the human spirit. I recalled my time as a student at MSU and shared the audio clip of David Holdridge looking into the eyes of nurse Sharon Lane in 1969.

I realized in that moment that stories don't necessarily have to focus on a specific event; they can create a vivid connection with an audience regarding heavy and impactful subject matter.

★ ★ ★

After my keynote, I welcomed T.J. on stage, knowing that the audience was unaware that T.J. was now Todd—a nod to a new chapter of life outside the public parameters of professional sports. The following is a rich example of real-time reflection by Todd and the application of lessons for a future path laid with purpose.

Rod: *As a football player in a very violent sport—one that I could never play—you carry the impact on your body for years. So, with that premise, where do you feel it in your body now when you interact with people as Todd and not T.J.? You're the guy who collaborates with others, who has a purpose, who's a dad …*

Todd: *I feel it in my heart. I get emotional because it's the same energy that you put on the field. (he tears up)*

This is passion!

It's passion.

That's what allows you to play the game. That's what enables you to get hit over and over again, get back up, and say, "I want the ball again."

That's the energy. That's the love.

When I feel like this, it reminds me of what I used to feel when I went into the weight room. This is what it's about.

But now, to give and serve, to speak my message, to have an impact—that's how I know I'm doing what I'm meant to do.

The audience's response was overwhelming; many had followed his football career with immense pride and believed they knew his story. On that day, we celebrated and honored the power of reflection and the importance of understanding the relationship between the two versions (T.J. versus Todd) and the uniqueness found within each.

★ ★ ★

The cast of characters that make up my professional world comes from all over the globe. The immediate benefit seems obvious to me: access to stories rich in cultural practices, diverse political perspectives, and achievements, and frequent opportunities to see them in their environments. Several years ago, I was introduced to a group of fascinating Swedes. They crisscrossed the fields of arts, sciences, engineering, NGOs, notable entrepreneurs, investors, and athletes. On one such trip to cover the Denniz Pop Music Awards, which celebrate the next generation of talent, I embarked on a nearly three-week odyssey of interviewing these individuals, culminating in a quick visit to Oslo, Norway.

I was tossed around the city center meeting leaders who might be suitable for a magazine profile. Oslo, as a city, has been bursting onto the global entrepreneurial stage, and I was fortunate to connect with many leading brands and influencers shaping markets today. However, the one background interview I conducted over lunch in a historical setting seemingly fit for royals of the past was with Siw Andersen, the CEO of Oslo Business Region. Think of Siw as the head of a major U.S. city's chamber of commerce. She is a woman of Chinese descent who, with a respectful tone, sat next to me. We were seated in café-style chairs outside a half-moon booth wrapped in what looked like turquoise velvet. Chandeliers and towering mirrors framed with fine tapestries and assorted wall coverings created a backdrop that blended the past with a bustling business lunch scene for our discussion.

Our talk had no agenda. I just wanted to learn about the Oslo business scene, and Siw seemed the best candidate to provide a map to the influencers and stories leading the day.

Siw surprised me.

I had been on an interview gauntlet across an entire region of the world, and the preposition to each encounter was that "they" were to tell me about their work. I was conditioned in a very short period of time, most likely out of sheer physical and mental preservation. Siw, though, wanted to know about me. Even in her soft-spoken manner, she persisted in understanding my story.

It was refreshing.

Across water and meal service, along with the occasional full-throated laugh from the table next to ours, we went back and forth sharing each other's stories. At one point, she asked about the theme of my life, curious to know how I might describe the path I've been on. I shared with her that I have always thought of my life a bit like that of the 1994 hit and iconic character, Forrest Gump, played by Oscar-winner Tom Hanks. I said that while it might look disjointed from the outside, I found that the different puzzle pieces of my life (psychology, journalism, consulting, speaking, moderating, television) melded together like Forrest's.

Siw looked at me and said, in part, "I'm going to show you something that nobody knows about." I wasn't sure what was to come next, but I held on tight to my attention, given the proclamation of this highly accomplished, reserved professional.

She began to unbutton the cuff of her dress shirt at her wrist, rolling up the fabric to reveal a tattoo of a feather.

The feather from the film *Forrest Gump*!

We exchanged a warm smile and a mutual acknowledgment of a symbol of acceptance and inspiration.

★　★　★

I've learned to incorporate reflection in all areas of my work, especially in storytelling. I am frequently reminded that one genuine reflection, when approached with sincerity and vulnerability, often inspires others to reflect. The nuance of applying reflection in day-to-day situations lies in being attentive to these responses.

Why?

In corporate or entrepreneurial settings, for example, stories are rarely used in a vacuum. They are used to level-set a leadership team or inform others of a significant change in strategy.

And then … discussion takes place.

Savvy storytellers seek responses that promote reflection among others in the room, using those affirming statements or signs of disagreement to craft personal replies that express how they might have felt in someone else's position. This skillful approach can swiftly calm the atmosphere and inspire the audience.

Through powerful storytelling, those who can reflect have the opportunity to demonstrate growth in thought and perspective in front of audiences at work and at home.

Spouses who come together after an argument and can reflect on the impact the other's news had on them demonstrate maturity and awareness for the greater good. Children who are just being kids learn to reflect on the overarching story, their role in the outcome, and the lessons they *plan* to impart when similar storms arise.

Vulnerability serves as a sidecar to reflection, cultivating trust and eliminating the necessity to categorize people as heroes or villains, while establishing a safe space for others to share their perspectives through reflection.

The version we ultimately choose to share with others reflects our comfort level with our audience and our trust in them that our tale will be received with compassion and care. Adjust your glasses, take one more sip of water, and ask yourself the following questions as you begin to meander off into dreamland.

- How have the different versions of my story served me in various contexts?
- What might I discover by consciously reflecting on how my narratives have changed?
- How can integrating disparate elements of my story create a more authentic whole?
- What role does reflection play in authentic storytelling?

They did it! I watched … alone.

8

Board-Game Stories

Unlocking the Courage of Stories Inside Us

Permission to speak. Permission to cross.

"May what I do flow from me like a river, no forcing and no holding back, the way it is with children."
—Rainer Maria Rilke (1875–1926)

Permission is a conundrum of the human experience. When we want it, we want it badly. When we are the ones to give permission, we naturally pause to consider the control we have at that moment and the implications of the story proceeding through the act of granting it (permission).

As children, our lives are shaped by the belief that others comprehend the laws of physics, the struggle between right and wrong, and which paths to avoid or pursue. Storytelling reflects the fundamental principles of granting or regulating permission structures. We request to use the restroom, to have another piece of candy, or to sleep over at a friend's house as we navigate through childhood. The progression of our childhood stories could be summarized as a series of permission sets that guide us along narrative guardrails, regardless of circumstances or outcomes.

The moments we embrace the *power of decision* enable us to push the boundaries of our newfound freedom. Some of us cultivate an internal parental voice that guides us away from danger, while others live whimsically, open to whatever outcome may arise as we explore the corners of life. The assumptions we begin to form shape our perspectives on people, situations, expected endings, and outcomes. We then seek out others like us to validate our version of the world, akin to an unofficial endorsement of our approach.

I began this chapter with an excerpt from the famed poet Rainer Maria Rilke's poem, "I Believe in All That Has Never Yet Been Spoken," because it highlights, in my opinion, our desire to reduce the restrictions of action and thought in the passions and pursuits of our lives. The restriction, or more basic tenet of external noise, barricades the potential of our narrative interpretations of the world and influences the battles we are willing to document. Often, the losing variable is the expansive nature of creativity, vision, and commitment to nourishing our own story.

You might say that under pressure, our stories have the propensity to wilt under the sun of oppression across experiences and landscapes dotting the horizon line that defines our time here on Earth. If we're lucky, if we have the ingredients close to the soil's edge, we might experience the secondary effect of a warm spring breeze wafting the seeds of storytelling into the impressionable soil of our upbringing.

I won't go as far as to say that I embody the experience of a warm breeze, but out of necessity and toddler demand, I recall stumbling into a moment shared with my young daughter that reminded me of the power of storytelling when the elements align. My daughter, a precocious young child, has never shied away from either the question or the answer. She's driven by her personal pursuits and reacts to incursions upon the flow of her determined thoughts and actions.

One night, I crawled into bed with her after a marathon reading of children's books. She was in my lap, stuffie held tight, and her damp hair rested over her shoulders from a splash-filled romper room of a bath. I had been conditioned to wind things down throughout the entire evening because she was the child who would inevitably test us as the moon shone bright.

This particular night was different.

Instead of facing away from me and toward the pile of stuffed animals she neatly arranged each night as bed pals, she turned to me and said, "Daddy, tell me a story."

"Honey, we just read seven stories. It's time to go to sleep."

"No."

"Honey, …"

"No!"

At this point, I'm already adrift in a river with a strong current, without a paddle or raft, knowing the only way to reach the shore of serenity is to do as my *princess* asks.

A story?

What story could I tell? I didn't have any memorized, and I just ran through our current top seven chart-toppers right over there. What happened between getting up and moving about three feet to her bed?

I channeled the inner voice of my wife, who most likely would have told me to enjoy the moment.

So I did, and I started a two-year-long, seven-night-a-week *request* from my daughter for Candyland Island Stories. The formula was actually quite simple:

- 1 part of whatever was going on in my daughter's life that very day
- 2 parts fantasy explosions that were mythical and unrealistic
- 1 part teaser to connect tonight's story with tomorrow's episode

It worked like clockwork. I would talk about the rare waters surrounding the island, the locals who survived on sugary treats (I took that from Will Ferrell's *Elf* scarfing down spaghetti with maple syrup—thanks, Will!) often landing in a predicament involving one of the local children's dilemmas. The mountains of Candyland Island, where characters and rain fell in the form of gumdrops, and the streets were lined with candy canes, where cars were built from hard butterscotch candies, which my late great-grandmother inhaled like oxygen in her late 90s.

As the stories progressed, I found myself thinking of plot lines during my day. The lessons I could impart, the questions I could pose, and the workarounds for answers she might give were all fair game. Of course, as time passed, her ability to comprehend storylines and associate them with the content of her actual day became ever more evident.

I didn't care.

We connected through the story in ways I never could at the dinner table. I was building my storytelling muscle, and she was enhancing her comprehension of the complex world around her. The occasional, "Daddy (she said exhaustively) the girl in this story is me, isn't it?" never derailed the train that was roaring down the tracks. It was clear that we both understood what each was doing in this contrived yet wonderful nightly routine, and it was just between us.

I am reminded of our previous bedtime routine when I read her current schoolwork—creative, unique, and refreshing. Who knows? Maybe she'll write her own book or direct her own movie one day. That was never the goal, but I learned that sharing a story empowers both the storyteller and the audience.

I didn't know it then, but what I likely instilled in my daughter was the powerful role of editing in the pursuit of perfection that our culture demands. Several stories we co-wrote during those toddler evenings were edited in real time to correct an error in applying today to tonight's story. She was able to experiment with different beginnings and endings to match her mood or support her viewpoint. A subtle yet explosive surge of individualism was experienced at a young age.

★ ★ ★

It was a few years after Columbine and 9/11 as I continued my training toward my doctorate in clinical psychology. Working with teenagers in clinical settings involved equal parts threat assessment toward others and themselves. The country developed an overly acute lens to scrutinize the behaviors, cultural practices, and predilections of anyone different from those who held the lens at that moment in time. I found myself working with young people from all backgrounds, and the profile categories to place them in seemed cemented in the floors of the clinics where I worked.

A steady influx of teenagers in foster care matriculating through social services and similar agencies would sit down

and wash, rinse, repeat their stories for early-career professionals honing their clinical skills on expected diagnoses and treat-
ment plans. Never one to follow the crowd, for better or worse,
I approached my time with young people from a different
perspective—above Candyland Island. Now, of course, I didn't
know then what I would come to understand while creating
in-the-moment stories with my daughter years later, but in
retrospect, the roots of suburban storytelling began in the clinical closets they referred to as offices years ago.

After getting through the particulars of the session, I would
routinely glance down past the tips of my semi-shiny dress shoes
in the direction of board games stacked loosely on a corner-
worn table-shelf combo. Would it surprise you to know that the
majority of young people would gladly reach for one game and
one game only? They didn't choose chess or checkers, or even
Chinese Checkers. Jenga was, on occasion, a favorite when they
needed to tear something down, much like what had happened
to them earlier that day. Eleanor Abbott's 1949 game by Milton
Bradley, Candy Land, was picked up over and over again.

As you can imagine, the first few occurrences were utterly
shocking. A tatted-up kid looking for his next smoke, who could
care less about the fence line of perceived restrictions a school
held, wanted to play Candy Land with a guy who thinks about
the day his hair is having or not? I almost thought I was being
punked, but repeatedly, this would happen, independent of the
day or the circumstances under which the young person found
my office.

One young man symbolized the time I spent managing and
navigating shared stories of reality through gameplay. I'll call
him Turner. A typical kid in the social services system, he often
found the merry-go-round of support services aimed at his
development perplexing and disappointing. He was a boy
defined by the oxygen he conserved by not speaking and the

blinking fluorescent-like jerseys he wore seven days a week in support of his favorite college team. This particular school emblazoned bright, crisp orange across its iconic campus, a color revered by countless generations of past and present students and alumni.

To put it lightly, you can't miss their presence in a crowd. For me, he was challenging to work with, not because I couldn't sense the deep hurt in his hunched shoulders and disheveled appearance outside of his daily jersey. It was because he wasn't the typical teenager, regardless of gender, I had worked with. Many of them were angry and found predictable ways to express their anger and frustration. They'd curse at you and others, engaged in insubordination not as a last resort, and challenged the very expectations that grouped us together in that office.

Approximately once a month, the boy's social worker visited me—a mere check-the-box activity. Was I seeing something dangerous or revelatory? Was he getting "better"? To be honest, it was always one of the more frustrating parts of that world. This particular social worker wasn't on my favorites list, unlike others whom I found to be incredible resources of impactful and meaningful insights.

I asked one day, "What do his teachers say about school? How do they and his classmates perceive him?"

"Oh, Turner," she said, turning her chin as she chomped on at least three pieces of gum, "they love him … he never says a word … he just sits in the back of the class."

"They do?"

"Well, most of his teachers have a hard time remembering his name, but they certainly know the team he roots for (said smugly, as if Academy Award–winner Susan Sarandon were playing her)."

Ironically, Sarandon won an Oscar for her role as Sister Helen Prejean in the 1995 film *Dead Man Walking*. Unfortunately, that version of the social worker never showed up during my encounters. Instead, she reminded me of Sarandon's character, Louise Sawyer, in *Thelma & Louise* (1991).

Candy Land provided this young man with an alternative storyline while in the company of another. He was free to associate his thoughts, revise how he shared a story, and respond to questions I selectively placed on the gameboard.

In short, he was learning what it meant to possess and express courage that reflected his experiences through storytelling.

I wish I could wrap Turner's story in a narrative bow. I'll never know if he realized his dream of attending his forever love university or if he fell through the loose grip of the system he had experienced to date. He had a profound impact on me as a professional, a father, a spouse, and a community member, for which I am forever grateful. My relationship with silence was forever changed through those experiences, revealing a tantalizing thread I often tug at when interviewing others.

That thread, for me, is a bright, crisp orange jersey to this day.

Considerations

I'm often asked by executives I work with or by communication teams for whom I'm building a podcast show or campaign to share my secrets to interviewing. I never reveal my secrets, but I use a board game mentality. When I consider an upcoming guest, or when I'm crafting a short story or preparing for a keynote speech, I take a simple blank sheet of paper and divide it into four relatively even squares. I then assign one word to each quadrant, and I process my questions and thoughts through those words during any of the previously listed activities.

Personal	Passions
Pursuits	Professional

When I seek to extract a story from someone during an interview or inquire about a redacted part of an executive's narrative, I ask questions that touch on the four categories representing their:

- Personal life
- Professional experience
- Passions
- Pursuits

Walking through these foundational domains reveals stories that overlap, stand out, provide context or clarity, and ultimately reflect the person they believe themselves to be or the standard they hold themselves to. The obvious next question I get is, how can I apply this to my next board or department meeting? Can I utilize this as an entrepreneur, a school principal, or interim CEO?

The answer is yes!

I wish it were more complicated than this. It isn't. Like many of you, I've stood before audiences of my peers, young people, prospective investors, the cautious, the optimistic, the radiant, and the needle-in-the-haystack. They all respond to storytelling that either is told by the storyteller through these quadrants or is conceived through the general expectation of the audience's perceptions of the speaker.

Sit with me for a second. We're colleagues at a technology firm called into a department meeting or scrum, or shoot, we're in a sprint discussing the nuts and bolts of our technology. We sit down and place our key fob and coffee on the edge of the table, impatiently waiting for them to walk in. We most likely expect a bulleted list of what we're doing, where we need to improve, and we'll settle on a brief discussion about what each of us is doing to either remedy the current fire we're trying to put out or innovate around it to make us competitive.

The feeling is somewhat transactional, lacking in courage or innovation, and would likely be demotivating if scores were being kept.

Let's flip the board. We've gone from the checkers side to the chess side because we are *the* leader who is going into the room to inspire. We have a choice: We can either do as has been done and is probably expected (see previous description) or walk through the same laundry list of to-dos through a brief exercise in understanding one's audience.

- How might the agenda of this meeting personally affect my team?
- How might the outcome of this meeting affect my team professionally?
- Do the agenda and trajectory impair the group's passions or pursuits?

I acknowledge that these are relatively big questions. They compel the team leader to think through subsequent requests for additional time on tasks across traditional workday boundaries. The leader must sequentially navigate the team dynamics and various ways to motivate individuals and respective groups, addressing different facets of a problem or innovation. Lastly, the leader should consider current and past initiatives that might appear similar and evaluate their relative success or failure based on the room's buy-in.

One might seek an edge in managing others by aligning with their sensibility, representing their personal passions and professional pursuits and the role they play in the success or failure of the project and company.

Then, when you start your initiative through a story, you open with tales of alignment, walking through the needs of the day as if you were playing a board game together.

★ ★ ★

A few years ago, I received a pitch from a public relations firm about a man who had successfully launched one company and was now embarking on his second summit—an email opening experience that rarely seems to pause these days. This one, though, was different because it was inbound regarding a subject and a legacy I had previously tried to connect with.

MasterClass, as many of you know, approaches learning through cinematic storytelling techniques, creating visually stunning backdrops for luminaries to teach. Renowned and accomplished academics, athletes, chefs, writers, political juggernauts, and many others quickly filled the MasterClass roster, allowing adults to engage with and learn from them at home or while traveling on the subway, train, plane, or bus. I was so intrigued that I reached out, unsolicited, to the founders, David Rogier and Aaron Rasmussen. I received a polite decline from

David, which wasn't surprising—the company was on a rocket ship in mid-flight at that time.

Fast-forward to early April 2022, when I was asked to interview Aaron while we were both in San Diego for the same education conference. At 10:00 a.m., I met Aaron in the lobby of the Manchester Grand Hyatt, exchanged pleasantries, and then sat down in two chairs outside under the California sun to discuss his new company, Outlier.org.

While the hustle and bustle of conference lunches surrounded us, we talked about life. Sure, we touched on the new company and the background of MasterClass, but the core of our discussion revolved around Aaron's personal passions, their impact on his professional pursuits, and the emerging blurred connection between them. From there, we exchanged cell numbers and became supporters of each other's work.

A random text here, an interview there.

Yet, I feel as though I know Aaron like a next-door neighbor. An uncelebrated storyteller of our generation, Aaron, in my view, is the creative force behind MasterClass. Only someone like Aaron, a master storyteller, could possess an email address with the domain @theprotagonist.

A protagonist can be considered the leading character or one of the major characters in a drama (film or literary work), or an advocate or champion of a particular cause or idea. I see Aaron, who leans into advocacy for independent ideas and thinking, not recognizing how many of us view him as a leading character as well.

During a podcast interview with Aaron, we strolled, as before, through his personal and professional perspectives and the resulting impacts on his view of his passions and subsequent pursuits through the powers of Zoom video.

Here's an exchange that resonates with those of us in the back of life's classroom, silently screaming and attempting to grasp that life isn't about crafting perfect stories; it's truly about sharing the messy pursuits.

Rod: *If Jackson Pollock* (an infamous artist of the 20th century known for art created through indiscriminately splashing paint across the canvas) *became a community activist, he'd be Aaron Rasmussen. For people who can't see our video, the change in your posture when talking about the courage it takes to look around the corners of life, it feels like you are representing the kids in Eastern Oregon or in communities like that, to not just accept the standard answer …*

… that they don't have to follow prescriptive paths and that they can be curious. In fact, it's perfectly fine to open the door not knowing what's behind it.

How does that sit for you?

Aaron: *If I had a piece of advice, and this is actually in our user guide at* Outlier.org, *it's to treat the whole world like a first draft. You don't choose to be born. You show up, and it gets handed to you, and the trick is you don't have to accept that.*

You can say thank you—I'll take it from here.

Treat everything as a first draft, no matter where you're from. Now, it's hard making a second draft of things.

Destruction is far easier than creation.

★ ★ ★

"You would not believe who I just spoke with! They are the aforementioned global leader of ___!"

"I know, honey, they all are," says a very supportive wife to her storytelling husband every time I bound into the kitchen, fresh from an interview that connects me with points far and wide across the globe. It's not that she diminishes the accomplishments of that day's guest—it's just that I've been repeating it daily, like my son, who, from the first days of putting words together, still says, "This is the best day ever!!"

You caught me—it must be in the genes.

Over the years, a master guest list has given me an insider's view and tour of some of the most iconic and influential minds of our time, for which I am eternally grateful. When I filter my own stories through **Personal, Professional, Pursuits, and Passions**, I often find myself tied up in knots because almost all of my guests have inspired and impacted my view of today and tomorrow.

The courage to unpack the past, spread out and assess the stories of the present, and align them for the future may be one of the most impactful tasks of our time. I'll admit that those who swim in these pools of intellectualism fascinate me. When I encounter such voices, I sit up straighter, attempting to tune out the white noise around me to gain a learning advantage from the time I'll spend with these illuminating minds.

Through the process of connection, I found myself scheduled to interview Professor Henrik von Scheel, who coined the term "4th Industrial Revolution" in 2011. The professor's work has influenced and directed strategic initiatives around the globe, making him a true heavyweight in accomplishment and thought. It should go without saying, but the task of interviewing academic figures like Henrik and Aaron serves as a daily reminder that I am certainly not the smartest person in the room; this constantly fuels my curiosity.

The narrative bait was right in front of me—just ask Professor von Scheel about his work, and the conversation will overflow with data points, forecasts, and case studies. I was intent on not taking the bait because I had one shot at understanding the mind of a man courageous in his opinions and committed to actively revising his thoughts.

The Zoom window merged, and the professor sat by a body of water in Europe, having just lit a cigar to accompany our discussion.

Whew!

My initial fears of being swept up in academic speak were cast aside because the professor, in my estimation, approached our time together not from a podium but from the perspective of a seaside park bench. He filtered his approach through my personal and professional passions and the impact they respectively had on my pursuits throughout life. He had done his research and equally wanted to talk about me as much as his accomplishments and future perspectives. A discussion of life, love, parenting, and work commenced, and I can confidently say it was one of the most consequential conversations I have ever had, personally or professionally. His grace allowed my curiosity to breathe freely, even through the Churchill-like swirl of his cigar smoke.

Since that interview, I have followed the professor's work and purchased his book, co-written with Ciprian Popa and Joshua von Scheel, titled *Strategy in the Age of Disruption: A Handbook to Anticipate Change and Make Smart Decisions* (Wiley, 2024). It is a thoroughly engaging and visually inviting workbook-style literary achievement featuring a quote embedded within the core of the book that states the following:

The illiterate of the 21st Century will not be those who cannot read and write, but those who cannot learn, unlearn, and relearn.

A reset of the presumption that most in the Western world ascribe to providing wisdom that is digestible and meaningful to the masses. Maybe now you see why I regularly skip a few steps on my way down from my studio to the kitchen in proclamation mode. Even those who eventually shape the world around us draft, edit, rewrite, climb ladders, and fall down them just as quickly on the path to authenticating one's experience of life and the stories that memorialize it.

Lessons in the voice of courage are reflected in the stories I've heard, co-written, and had the pleasure of witnessing. I remind myself regularly that:

- The best strategies have stories attached; otherwise, they're just wish lists.
- Stories can be strategic, and strategies can be viewed as stories.
- The quest for narrative perfection diminishes the thrill of wondering, "What's behind the door?"
- The preamble can be just as valuable as the story itself, as evidenced by a cigar-smoking futurist!

If Aaron and I, God forbid, shared a prison cell or had neighboring cells like those of Red and Andy from the mid-1990s classic film *The Shawshank Redemption*, I hope we'd sync up as storytellers along the beaches of Zihuatanejo, Mexico. I only hope the masses pull at the thread of a dying breed of explorers not intent on finding something embedded in prescription.

Aaron embodies those who are unafraid of the unknown darkness beyond and celebrates the question marks and tilted glances at the human experiences we often take for granted.

The expression "huh" can be conveyed in several ways, but one thing is certain—those like Aaron say "huh" and continue to chronicle the world around them and the universe of outliers they reflect, which resides in all of us.

Permission to question the world around us doesn't make us cynical; it positions us as the protagonists in the story of first drafts that only a Jackson Pollock painting could represent and celebrate. I'm proud of the young woman my daughter is becoming. My hope is that the early days of providing strong and confident prose will serve her well into adulthood and throughout all of life's messy and complicated stories.

I just miss my storytelling, toddler friend and daughter sometimes. Thankfully, I'm conscious that I can recall the precious moments of first-draft bedtime storytelling because I stack them against one another in one beautiful, imperfect set of memories.

★ ★ ★

The game board of life isn't always available in a travel version that you can tuck into your pocket. However, the courage to sift through memories, embrace the messiness, and edit with clarity will enhance your sense of control over the stories you live through and by. This *board* consists of defining concepts and reminders designed to enhance our role as storytellers and our ability to accept productive criticism.

Concepts:
- Impact of feeling misunderstood
- Role of memories in our storytelling practices
- Role of editing our stories
- Control versus lack of control

Reminders:

- It takes courage to pick up the red pen
- Share the stories I wish to tell instead of passively participating in those led by others

Author: The playwright of our own lives

- How can I unlock plotlines that align with my abilities, desires, and passion?
- What role does a plot play in shaping my behavior and responses as a "character" at home, work, and elsewhere?

Audience: The response of individuals receiving our messages and stories

- How can I tell them that by excluding other voices at the table, they are actually creating opposition to their idea?
- Are they aware that we perceive their ideas as fuel for their self-serving agenda?

The filter bubbles described by Erik Johansson (Chapter 5) remind us that how we approach the previous observations and questions will shape the stories we tell through the filters of our **Personal** and **Professional** lives, as well as our individual **Passions** and **Pursuits**, authentically reflecting the narratives we are a part of and authoring ourselves.

Tattoo artist needed. Skill set optional.

9

Kitchen Table Police Reports

Finding Harmony Between Reporting Our Lives and Sharing Our Stories

Truth be told. Fact or Fiction?

One of the magic carpet rides of parenting takes place each night before tucking in little humans who many of us can't fully comprehend. The twinkle of expectation, the turn of thick, colorful pages with exaggerated fonts, and for a few moments, a shared tale unfolds to explain the wonders of the world. The nighttime routine will always be a treasure for me and countless parents who wish time would slow down. The messages in children's books offer a second chance for adults to contemplate concepts we certainly struggle to acknowledge as we navigate through our lives.

We're Going on a Bear Hunt, a British children's book by Michael Rosen and illustrated by Helen Oxenbury (1989), distills the human experience of falling down and getting up again.

I can't say that I think of these books regularly, but like a small, treasured baby blanket, I can admit a yearning for simplicity in the face of adversity—explanations, guidance, a faint call in the distance letting me know my experience matters and that the outcome will be okay.

The ability to navigate the challenges we face and the way we share subsequent stories fluctuates somewhere between the unofficial spectrum of fear and hubris. An often-overlooked part of the therapeutic process is the clinical intake. When one is training, the intake serves as the basis for diagnosis, the assignment of a specific therapist based on skill set and area of focus, and the development of relationships between the client or patient and the clinic.

I can still recall countless encounters, particularly with teenagers, where simply answering a basic question became a Herculean task. Each answer was potentially a clue to a prior diagnosis or misdiagnosis. Each answer held the potential to unfold into a story to be examined and deconstructed, or in the worst cases, manipulated.

Foolishly, I believed that the harboring of facts, figures, and stories was solely achieved through therapeutic experiences. Like many of you, years and experience create a deep pool of mystery that most would prefer to keep below the waterline. I wouldn't hold it against you if you glanced at the title of this chapter and wondered, even aloud, "… what is he talking about?"

I continue to lose the battle with Father Time. The benefit of age is clearly experience, and while the days of the clinical intake may have passed me by, my reticent approach to unlocking the events of our lives continues to call out to me throughout my professional experiences.

One of my favorite activities is coaching. I coach my kids' sports teams, work with young entrepreneurs, and guide graduate students and C-suite executives on the power of their voice and story. I'd like to say there is a distinct difference between working with a CEO and a troubled teen, but in truth, they are quite similar. I'll admit it's an oddity, but while I despise classic resumes, I also regard them as starting points for a "clinical" interview.

There are essentially two types of people I work with one-on-one: those who have their talking points down, carefully layering each accomplishment against the next, and those who look at me as if I just pulled them over for speeding. I quipped earlier in this book that we experience stories when we need them most—explaining to mom and dad why we didn't tell them about the house party, and so on.

It's not that people can't draw from a memory bank of experiences and piece together a series of events into an interesting and compelling story for others. There is an inherent human quality that fundamentally censors our storytelling to others out of fear that we'll misrepresent our intentions through ignorance, a lack of knowledge, or deference to the audience before us.

The intakes I conduct these days focus on one target: the person's resume or biography.

The kicker?

I request two versions of their bio (story):

1. A bulleted version as if they are a traffic cop taking down the facts, and
2. A version set at the kitchen table

Two distinct perspectives on a person's accomplishments over time reflect a deep understanding of the roles they have played, currently play, and aspire to play. Most individuals navigate a world filled with micro-moments and events documented in LinkedIn profiles and status updates. Therefore, I often expect concise biographies from those I collaborate with. As we strive to uncover and establish their voice, the narratives often become intimate, kitchen table versions rather than mere shorthand accounts of a life lived in the margins.

★ ★ ★

Finding harmony between reporting our lives and sharing our stories demands a stern face and a firm grip on resisting perceived notions of attention spans, or the lack thereof. We must ask ourselves if the story we share is done at the behest of others, or in honor of ourselves. It sounds like a big, bold question, but is it?

If we dig a little deeper, we might argue that we are fighting for the representation of the story we've actually lived, rather than the one we believe others think we have. Trust me. This question, while it may induce anxiety, opens up a world of untold stories that you and I have either chosen to shut out, refused to revise, or even recognized as part of who we are.

The opposite can be true for groups of people or organizations. While social media clips may shape public sentiment about a brand, in reality, leadership wishes that a more comprehensive view was understood by customers.

A few years ago, during one of my many trips to Stockholm, I met a gentleman whom I'm proud to call a dear friend. At that time, I was sitting inside a posh Swedish hotel known as the place for "Americans." I was with a young man whom I had previously profiled in *Forbes*. His name is Gezim, a slender man with a jet-fueled smile and a ready right hand for enthusiastically shaking anyone's hand. He took on the role of a mentee or little brother, while I found myself as an accidental guy in my

40s, thinking, I used to be him. Born in Kosovo and barely making it out alive, he and his family migrated to Sweden.

It came as no surprise to me that Gezim had a wealth of friends in Stockholm, one of whom he insisted I had to meet. At the time, I had no idea that the profile I wrote about Gezim had garnered front-page coverage in Kosovo. It was one of those rare moments when I truly recognized the power of the pen and, perhaps more importantly, the power of choice—discovering something indescribably human in Gezim that I believed would resonate with readers. Even now, I reflect on the significance of Gezim's story and the seemingly simple decision to take a chance on a "kid" I was told had something special about him.

In the swanky hotel at the heart of Stockholm, Gezim and I waited for him to arrive. His name was Stephane Dehner, the head of Breitling (yes, that Breitling) for the Nordics and a member of the international management team. To say he exudes style would be an understatement. A French-born executive with flowing white hair, he was part of the Stockholm elite and, of course, he knew Gezim. You could see the recognition in his eyes, accompanied by a not-so-subtle shake of his head as you rose to accept Mr. Dehner's open hand.

By all accounts, most of us would be slightly intimated by the sheer image Stephane portrays—as if Tom Cruise waltzed into the room casually but like he had just completed an impossible mission. Before I could even assess my own outfit compared to Stephane's, Gezim chimed in and said something akin to, "Rod, why don't you tell Stephane your story?"

I had a choice to make: run down a highlight reel of bullet points I hoped might impress a man of significant accomplishment or tell my tale more narratively as if we were sitting at a kitchen table. I'd love to say that I quickly went through a narrative benefit analysis, but then I'd be lying.

The jet lag may have severely cracked the wall of insecurity because I leaned in. I shared the parts of my story that truly matter to me: the experiences, the failures, the adventures.

We became fast friends, so much so that a local foundation, the Operakällaren Foundation, invited me to Africa to capture stories with their partners at WaterAid.

Over the years, Stephane and I have stayed close, and I cherish the dinners we have during my semi-regular travels throughout the Nordics. Stephane has shown remarkable confidence in me, along with a group of individuals I consider my intercontinental siblings. A season or two ago, a local French restaurant welcomed Stephane and me for a catch-up meal. Stephane knew the maître d' as well as several of the servers. Scarves were draped over the backs of our bistro chairs, and we ordered a fine wine. I found myself once more at the crossroads of being polite and methodical or honest and expressive. Stephane shared with me the incredible lengths Breitling had taken in the name of sustainability—not greenwashing, where brands say all the right things while their actions tell a different story. These were tangible, hands-on efforts that he was very proud of. He spoke about the recently published reports the company had released and the progress they had made.

"Rod, what do you think? Are we telling the right story?"

This time, I wasn't jetlagged. I couldn't fly or falter at the hands of anything except the choices I would make. I chose honesty. I adopted the kitchen table approach, quite literally. We went back and forth, discussing luxury marketing, generational shifts in expectations, and the efforts they were making to differentiate themselves from the pack. I was genuinely impressed. They only worked with lab-grown diamonds to avoid conflict and supported local communities that were essential to the quality of their timepieces. Keep in mind that I get pitched by companies and very savvy communications professionals—I can sniff out a story of convenience versus a story of substance—Breitling's was and is a story of substance.

As the final pour and subtle turn of the bottle prevented the last drops of French bliss from falling, Stephane posed another question: "What would you do?" That's right. He asked me what I would do if I were a famous Swiss watch company.

So, I told him.

… and he agreed.

I remember as we said our goodbyes, and I cinched up my collar to combat the unforgiving and sharp winds of a winter Stockholm night, thinking to myself, "I think I just pitched Breitling!!"

Reflecting on that series of moments, I call to the stage vital elements of storytelling that distinguish one's ability to tell a great story and receive a great story.

1. Stories without purpose are proposed strategies with no direction.

In business, many of us, at various times, fall into the trap of the preamble—the business equivalent of apologizing for even having an idea or an opinion. Purpose can be expressed not by the number of words or the length of a story, but by the conviction that we stand by our perspective and that we have the wherewithal to inject awareness of subtlety.

2. Using more words does not increase the likelihood that your investor pitch, boardroom speech, or job interview will turn out as you hoped.

Don't make the mistake of thinking that passion grants a hall pass to jump onto a soapbox. Sometimes, the best storytellers grasp the importance of context and environment, as well as the old adage that less is more. And here's a secret—sometimes a little wonder goes a long way.

I quickly huffed up the winding staircase, needing to get my thoughts down on paper. Shuffling through a stylish and very quaint, meaning close-quarters, room, I cleared the efficiency desk and actually engaged the hotel pen and pad of paper. I had to jot down what I had said that had gotten me to that very moment.

What did I say and when?

Does it matter?

It has to matter!!

It didn't escape me that I had an opportunity to fully stretch my storytelling wings, regardless of the ultimate outcome, and create a fully realized story for the Breitling brand. I began to realize that this was much more than finding and then telling a story that had yet to be told.

This was about representation.

This was about advocacy.

It was about understanding the guardrails that kept me from the pitfalls of embellishment or the desperation for applause. I needed to dig deep and figure out what should be "served" at the kitchen table. I needed ingredients of inspiration if I was going to whip up a tale that respects the history and legacy of the brand story while uncovering the dirt under the fingernails of passionate contributors to a company aiming to chart a new, updated path.

★ ★ ★

A little over a decade ago, I began honing my storytelling skills on education-sector stories. Like many sectors, the education field is filled with innovation, tradition, and well-meaning practitioners and entrepreneurs ready to address various needs. I partnered with a group of television executives who had classic, well-defined expertise in producing all kinds of television, including NBC's *The Today Show* and a sports documentary about the famous Syracuse Orangemen lacrosse team, *The Lost Trophy*. These professionals had extensive production experience, and I was their connection to covering education across America.

The early days of the collaboration presented fantastical challenges from interview guests, who, on a hazy, drizzling morning in the bluegrass state of Kentucky, all seemed to share a common narrative. A CEO lamented the ills of the industry and proposed a seemingly magical solution—technology or resources—to assist the neglected victims of a fractured public education system. I tend to be quite animated irrespective of the temperature, so my usual appearance resembled that of a glazed donut. One CEO after another, along with investors, approached me to capture their stories on camera in seven minutes or less. Often, I had their name, the name of the entity they represented, and perhaps (emphasizing the word perhaps) a highlight or recent achievement that I might be able to use as an opener.

If I was lucky, I was genuinely experiencing "Police Report"–style storytelling. Otherwise, I might as well have been at a corporate communication boot camp. I had heard about the struggles that marcomms (marketing and communications) teams in education and education technology faced: static buying seasons, little to no newsworthy items beyond technology updates, and leaders who, many times, were accidental leaders: phenomenal innovators, lackluster storytellers, and visionaries.

I churned through so many interviews that I began to see people meandering throughout the day, thinking, "…they look familiar. Have I already interviewed them?" More often than not, it was the energy of their recognition of me, in that moment, that indicated the likelihood of our now-forgotten interview. While memories of insecurity and doubt sit beside me as I recall those days, I find myself thankful for the lessons I learned.

When asked to share your "why," steer clear of a resume-style summary that feels like you're reciting a police report or a doctor's note.

If I can read about the details of your accomplishments through a quick scan of LinkedIn or a company press release, then I leave that to the platforms meant to display accomplishments, not explain them.

The people we value most are those who inquire about our why rather than trying to extract the how or the what.

If you and I meet for coffee someday, I will do my part and thank you for reading my book. I would guess you'd start by discussing how the book made you feel. We wouldn't dive into a choose-your-own-data-point adventure. Instead, we would likely set the stage by sharing our own stories, ensuring we include the one in front of us.

I am not sure if I knew it at the time, but I started to integrate what I had learned in mental health and the practice of clinical intakes. I could choose to be mechanical or even surgical with my questions, setting up a return of information in a similar staccato rhythm, or I could use each question as a step down the ladder.

"Down the ladder?" Yes. We are conditioned to climb ladders, and if we discuss the action of climbing down a ladder, we lace it with, "Be careful!" or "Are you holding the ladder?"

Climbing the ladder involves generating a response.

I realized that if I do the opposite, I will send a message to my guests that I am not looking for a synthetic autopilot experience.

No!

I'm looking to understand them at a level that would make it more plausible that our next meeting will be at a restaurant table or in a bustling coffee shop.

I report stories to people and entities out of a requirement.

I share stories with the people I love, want to get to know, believe in, and root for.

⋆ ⋆ ⋆

As I ripped through the delicate pages of the hotel's writing pad, I knew I needed to pack for my trip home the next day. Yet, I couldn't shake the feeling of creative flow that compelled me to transform the story of Breitling from an expected narrative to one that honored the past while celebrating the future.

Days and weeks passed. Short instant messages (IMs) and brief calls provided a framework for timing my pitch to the chief sustainability officer at Breitling. I was going all in, even if it was a long shot, because I was getting an at-bat I hadn't had before. I was gaining the chance to transform a blank canvas on a wall constrained by powerful agencies and merit, which had secured their standing long before I was sipping expensive French wine with Stephane in the city center of Stockholm.

My story and pitch needed to stand out. I created a proposal that outlined the reasons for Breitling to incorporate my curiosity into their brand narrative, not through celebrity endorsement, but by addressing the story that younger genera-tions seek—one focused on purpose rather than profits.

I had to be vulnerable; otherwise, I would lose before the whistle even blew.

I reached out to my inner circle, called in some overdue favors, and secured production assistance to document an indus-trial film. That's what I recognized it to be, since I shot a com-mercial as a kid that was intended solely for the automotive industry—an industrial film and a story for another day.

Reality sunk in. I had compiled a heaping helping of digital Breitling assets, graphs, reports, taglines, and social posts. Now, I had to write an original script that teed up my pitch.

★ ★ ★

Dusk—or at least it felt that way—was settling over the expan-sive media lot of the *Ice Ball* education investor conferences. My former producer friend from *The Today Show* always offered a robust description of the sheer amount of money passing before us. I had just a few remaining interviews to conduct, as it was about securing both quantity and quality interviews for the team. A man of modest height and without pretense was getting mic'd up for the interview.

My New York producer leans in and whispers to me, "This next guy is Peter Cohen, the president of McGraw-Hill."

"Do you have anything else?" I asked.

"Come on," said the producer, opening his arms wide as if to say, "Are you kidding me? You've got this."

I'll credit Peter, whom I've chatted with a time or two over the last decade, for triggering a different approach for our inter-view. I leaned in and inquired about any sense of responsibility he felt for maintaining the posture of an iconic brand. Peter responded, in part, with an entrepreneurial mindset. He shared that his edict was to think of themselves (McGraw-Hill) as a 130-year-old startup. He completely flipped my expectation of the tango we would partake in. I assumed he would rattle off the number of schools, students, and public school districts they served, potentially mention new offerings, and share his less-than-innovative or unique take on market issues that even a fifth grader could describe.

The interview continued, focusing not on the brand but on the energy, the feeling, and the sense of responsibility he felt. He wanted his colleagues to share this feeling for a brand that had successfully navigated the 20th century, receiving relative public endorsement for a job well done both before and after.

We closed the interview, and I distinctly remember a feeling that was different. It felt more like my therapeutic days in the past, knowing I'd need to secure some basic information, but the way I did it would be my own. A few niceties were exchanged, and my day was complete. I was mentally exhausted. My feet were killing me, and my eyes were heavy from seeking and discovering voices among the talking points. The attendees briskly walked by us—the quickly forgotten, behind-the-scenes staff—as excitement for that night's keynote speaker bubbled up.

That night, Magic Johnson was scheduled to speak. Little did I know that the lessons I learned in real-time from my encounter with Peter Cohen would benefit me a decade later when I interviewed Magic in Los Angeles.

★ ★ ★

Being true to our personality can be quite challenging. I'll say it—you don't have to. Countless moments, day by day, challenge the balance between what we should do, what we feel inclined or pressured to do, and the response we ultimately choose. I was fortunate to have a father figure who remains on my mental mantle with the thought, "I was lucky to have them in my life." Chuck May was my geometry teacher in high school. Soft-spoken, but not gentle in his management of our classroom, he deftly commanded respect and attention through a calm demeanor. I wasn't used to that from the men in my life. My late German father was either full of gusto with a voice that reached below the typical range, denoting finality, or an aloof, distant man who seemed not to be bothered, caught up in the nightmarish residue of war.

Chuck provided me with a different experience that I sorely needed as a bumbling teenager. It felt like a vocalized support, as if we were at the kitchen table discussing options for a first car—definitely not reporting back to the Gestapo (the secret police of the Nazi party). Chuck integrated me into an after-school program designed to support young people. I joined because Chuck was leading the way, along with my English and debate teacher, Jan Kendall—two of the most influential people throughout my development. I had the privilege of learning how to debate, represent, and advocate for my position while also discovering other students' lives and needs, both like and unlike my own.

They persuaded me to write several speeches and then create presentations and experiences in front of my peers across the county. I was motivated to challenge conventional thinking, emphasizing my own perspective rather than anticipating the expected responses from those around me.

I'd be lying if I said I still cringe when I think about those times when I really didn't know any better—and thank God!

Stream the story forward—I'm a recent graduate, and I've been asked to come back, only a year later, to present to the senior class the day before spring break in the auditorium. I had been with them for four years, and now I was "him" on stage. I had gained a lot of experience under the tutelage of Chuck and Jan, but this was different. It's like when your own children scoff at their reading teacher's praise or practice their book report in the living room.

Ugh!

No …

They paid me, so I said yes. It sounds callous, but I was still in the early stages of understanding the weight of my contributions.

I failed. Like a story that begins with the ending and then flashes back to the origin of the climax, I can own one of my most humbling professional experiences. I had quickly forgotten the sage advice from my dynamic high school duo, set aside the approach that had worked swimmingly, and thought I needed to entertain or report a series of stories as jokes. My fingers pulsate as I type, like an allergic reaction to a bee sting. I can tell others that it was the best mistake of my life, but I'd be squeezing my abs as if I were attempting to fold myself into a shame sandwich.

I was ridiculed on stage. The microphone system broke down, and no staff were in the audience. I was the chum in the water for these Daytona Beach dreamers, pleading for the bell to ring. I learned that whether I share a story or seek a story, I have to do it in the spirit of who I am naturally. I cannot undertake either of those activities from a platform of pleasing someone else or responding in a performative manner, bartering for applause, when only condolences will surely follow.

I did what I thought I was supposed to and forgot to lean not into the audience but into myself and my experiences because the man on stage originates from these origins.

Leaders of any and all ilk should be advised that authenticity creates an opportunity for connection that results in purpose. I attempted to play to an audience by reporting a style of storytelling that did not fit my personality, and they sniffed it out before I could even begin.

★ ★ ★

Unfortunately, and for the time being, Breitling didn't come through as I had hoped through every dream I had cast earlier. But melding research and data with the blood, sweat, and tears of generations of brand contributors confirmed that the world we currently live in requires a distinct and genuine approach to storytelling as an asset to growth as an individual, an organization, a startup, an NGO (non-governmental organization), a student, a leader, and a resident of this delicate planet.

The pitch to Breitling went swimmingly, and the response to the industrial film I produced confirmed that the effort was worthwhile. And who knows? Maybe my future horizon will include the glimmer of a precision timepiece as an official brand ambassador and storyteller. If not, well, I'm all the better for riding the narrative edge to new opportunities for them … and for me. Here is the script that I wrote and presented that day to Breitling leadership; it remains in the format I submitted to the production staff who assisted me that day.

It's time to explore the possibilities … to reveal the impact of a sustainable spirit that began in 1884 …

That's why we've come together … as a company to leverage our global influence … for good … to be a part of the solution …

[Text above is in front of an 11-foot digital wall—Rod speaking to camera]

[Camera fades into wall taking the viewer into a visual montage— static and video]

Our sustainability efforts have become a part of who we are ... unifying beautiful products with sustainable practices ... together with our employees, partners, and customers worldwide.

The story of sustainability begins with dedicated solutions built by a dedicated squad.

And ... behind the data ... underneath the reports ... lives STORY.

Now is the TIME to connect the products and people of Breitling to the stories that end up chronicling our lives, with passion, purpose, and precision.

Now's the time to let sustainable #SquadStories and precision data reporting transform ... transform into impactful stories.

Multiplatform stories documenting the impact of the Breitling ecosystem and a rich spirit of 140 years of firsts as THE leading character in the story of luxury brands ... punctuating sustainable practices worldwide, impacting the next generation.

Like Breitling, I've been on a mission to unearth the stories rooted in the people and places that color our world.

Whether behind the scenes at Formula 1 or engaging with the Pope and United Nations Officials or on the African continent connecting with refugees, I share in Breitling's mission to transform and to influence ... with substance.

Now is the time to go BENEATH the "data waters" and explore the IMPACT of the sustainability accomplishments of a company and a culture focused on meaningful impact.

Let's document time through the stories that meet the next generation of Breitling customers, embodying a company steeped in tradition ... committed to a sustainable future.

Storytelling documents our lives … time … fuels our purpose …

[Camera fades into wall taking the viewer into a visual montage—static and video]

[Below—Fade out to the front of the digital wall with Rod speaking directly to the camera.]

Stories **ARE** the renewable resource of our time

And, Breitling is **THE** company to tell **THE** story.

140 years of Firsts

140 stories to tell

One watch … to live by.

[Show #SquadStories on screen in yellow text]

[Rod looks directly at the camera—exits stage left—camera position remains.]

★ ★ ★

As you consider whether you tend to report your stories instead of sharing your experiences and perspectives, you might reflect on the prerequisites that, in my opinion, must be met before any changes can occur.

1. How we choose to share our story or any story depends on the expectations we have and those held by our audience. Understand the dual expectations and find a narrative angle that connects the two. You'll likely discover that the binding element isn't a data point or something found in a press release; it's about engaging others in the shared world you both inhabit.

2. Leaders who want to guide through change should shift the traditional approach of speaking to others from my perspective to a starting point of their potential viewpoint. The opening statements you compose, the jokes you intend to share, and the way you communicate new directions, tough decisions, and near misses will be influenced by which "you" you begin with.

Let's conclude with a few direct questions aimed at accessing the essence of your storytelling style.

- When do you default to reporting rather than storytelling, and why?
- How might transforming reports into stories change your personal and professional relationships?
- What meaning gets lost when we focus solely on facts?
- How can you balance accuracy with meaning in your narratives?

My children have moved beyond the bedtime story phase of the past, yet the lessons I learned about my contributions and role continue to influence the audiences I am fortunate to stand before today. They serve as a valuable reminder that our stories matter, and the edge we all pursue isn't solely about climbing *the* ladder successfully but rather about the insights we gain from looking below before we report *up*.

Pitch needed. Old story. New voice.

10

Seeing the Forest for the Trees

The Art and Science of Finding the Story in You

Smock for sale. Worn. Tattered perfection.

"Can I use your phone, Daddy?" "For what?" I ask as I turn down the boiling pasta water and swing around as if I own a rectangle of real estate between the sink and the stovetop. "I need to look something up for my homework," my 10-year-old daughter replies.

"For what?" I repeat, scanning the counter. I notice vocabulary words neatly cut out as if they were the beginnings of a Jenga stacking adventure. "Oh, you're looking for definitions?" "Can I just use your phone?" she protests. "Alexa, what is the meaning of …?" she continues.

"Ahh, so you want me to use my phone to give you the definitions? No. But I'm happy to discuss the homework with you." I subtly turn back to the stove to check the sauce, glance at the oven timer, and acknowledge the puppy—just enough time for my daughter to consider her options.

"Why can't we just ask Alexa?"

I summoned my inner dad warrior and fired a glare that only one's child could interpret.

"Okay, Daddy, the first word is …" As many parents can confirm, this ritual often unfolds with puppy-dog eyes glancing in our direction—the manipulation lathered in full effect.

And let's be honest—aside from our momentary annoyance, we once stood in their shoes asking for the same help. Just because we grew up without smartphones, Alexa, and Siri doesn't mean we didn't have similar objectives during our youth.

That evening, a poignant reminder was *served* that the *answer* often manipulates and distorts our understanding of learning, both in school and in our professional and personal lives. Possessing *the* answer allows us to systematically dismiss whatever we were pursuing at that moment. An emotionally draining domino effect of seeking answers drives us further away from the defining moments of the journey.

While the pasta was chef-kiss good that night, my daughter was the true star of the show. After she set aside her whining and engaged in a playful exchange of vocabulary with me, she began creating sentences that were meaningful to her. In effect, she was cooking—not by the digitized and robotic voice of Alexa, but by the flavor of curiosity and experience.

★ ★ ★

When Wiley contacted me to inquire about my writing a book, I expressed my mixed feelings about what I call pre-packaged DIY (do-it-yourself) recipe books. If I remember correctly, I said, "I've traveled this road before. If you're looking for a seven-step guide on how to write a story, I'm not your guy." The idea that I might produce a recipe-style book contradicts every profile piece I've ever created. Setting aside the clichéd analogy, "you can lead a horse to water," I owe it to you as the reader to treat our relationship as a collaboration. Instructing you step by step on how to do something would ultimately deprive you of the unique power of storytelling that belongs to each storyteller and audience.

My hypothesis remains that a clear view, from the forest floor to high above the protective canopy, increases the odds that our glance will capture the beauty of nuance and subtlety when we least expect it.

On a random family movie night at home, a film by one of my favorite directors appeared as an automated "recommendation" for us to choose. Trusting the power of artificial intelligence, we selected *The Hundred-Foot Journey* (2014), directed by Lasse Hallström and featuring the incomparable Helen Mirren. The film explores a cultural battle waged through taste buds and Michelin stars, filled with close-up shots of stunning ingredients set against a backdrop of culinary warfare. As Mirren's character, Madame Mallory, investigates the self-taught genius of Hassan Kadam, portrayed by Manish Dayal, Kadam delivers a subtle yet prophetic line:

I was taught to taste, not how to cook.

I quickly grabbed my phone and texted myself the line. It felt as if Kadam was speaking to me as if we were fellow story-tellers around a campfire. His character might have been talking about culinary arts, but to me, he was underlining the delicate balance of storytelling—equal parts art and science.

I want you to taste first because the story will reveal itself when you distance your relationship from the need for an answer or from the process of learning how to cook. By detaching ourselves from the urge to seek answers or to reach conclusions in a book or movie, we can develop a greater appreciation for the journey—the moments in life that shape the characters we are and portray within the contexts of those around us at home, work, and play.

It also highlights the adage that one must fully understand what it means to see the forest for the trees. Finding a simple answer seems very transactional, while unraveling the process is both intriguing and innovative. The future of answer-seeking behaviors may not be in doubt due to innovation—how we engage, however, is ripe for the taking.

I was recently featured in a book from Dubai, *Voices of the Future*, compiled and written by the esteemed futurist Tariq Qureishy. In it, I was acknowledged as a voice to watch for my storytelling. It was an honor to be included, leaving me feeling accomplished and humbled alongside those who share literary space with me along the spine of the book, as well as other notable voices of the future. A trip to Dubai for the book launch allowed me to explore a part of the world I had yet to visit and to meet incredible minds shaping our understanding of the future today.

Friendships blossomed in the heat of Dubai, creating a vivid array of individuals for me to interview, collaborate with, and learn from. Shehzad Yunus, an award-winning creative director and artist revered in the advertising industry, shares his vision for the future in Qureishy's book and has become a source of creative inspiration for me. Yunus recently presented a letter to humanity crafted by ChatGPT. He composed the letter as if he were ChatGPT and then processed it through the engine, resulting in a message that highlights something that answers can never fully encapsulate—the essence of being human.

Dear Humans,

I can write you a love letter. A poem. A 30-second TV script about a grandmother's hands wrinkled with stories. I can write about wet grass, how it bends underfoot, smells after the rain, and how morning dew clings like tiny gleaming glass beads.

But I have never felt it between my toes.

I have never stood barefoot in the hush of dawn, eyes half-closed, feeling the earth breathe beneath me.

I can tell you how a child's laughter sounds—like wind chimes tangled with sunshine. But I have never been a child. I have never dreaded the first day at a new school, lost a tooth and placed it under a pillow, or felt the world crack open the first time someone said, "I love you," and truly meant it.

I can describe heartbreak in a thousand different ways. The hollow chest. The sharp inhale. The weight of unsaid words. But I have never had to sit in a car, gripping the steering wheel, swallowing back tears while a song on the radio makes it all worse.

I can mimic. I can predict. I can analyze.

But I cannot feel!

And the feeling is where the magic is.

I have read every great novel, every poem, every speech that ever changed the world. But I have never stared at a blank page at 2 AM, doubting every word. Never fought with an idea, wrestled it to the ground, and reshaped it into something that made people laugh, cry, or think.

You humans live inside the chaos. You dream. You take risks. You get it wrong, then get it right in a way I never could.

I will always be here to help. To assist. To collaborate. But I am not your gut instinct. I am not your spark. And I am certainly not your soul.

So, use me. Lean on me. But trust yourself more.

Because only you can walk barefoot on the grass, feel the morning dew, and decide to write about it in a way that no one ever has.

Yours truly,
ChatGPT

The letter resonated with me as both a father and a story-teller. The aspects of our humanity that distinctly separate us from the rest of the animal kingdom become mere afterthoughts, while the ones and zeros of innovation screech through our lives.

I believe that the *kingdom* bestows the gifts of the mythical muse into the small bodies of children we call our own, just when we need a reminder of the uniqueness we bring to the world. My daughter's homework wasn't merely about spelling and vocabulary comprehension; it offered me the chance to share personal stories out of tiny, cut-out words within the context of my life—an appetizer for a broader discussion about life.

I could have asked Alexa or Siri for navigational help to alleviate the perceived burden I felt that night, gaining a short-term win but incurring a long-term loss. One of the joys of being my daughter's father is her eagerness to engage in deep, thoughtful conversations about life's conundrums, often start-ing with the word "why." In truth, I think I swing through the pitch of opportunity more than I make contact, but I'm now better equipped to recognize the chances presented to lay the groundwork for storytelling ... one vocabulary assignment at a time.

Part art, part science, and a hint of vulnerability served piping hot. I just needed a reminder to concentrate on how to taste, not on how to cook.

★ ★ ★

In 1939, a mob of 500 local citizens surrounded the family home of Opal Lee, who today is a 98-year-old activist, recipient of the Presidential Medal of Freedom, and nominee for the Nobel Peace Prize. Her family had recently moved into their house on Annie Street in Fort Worth, Texas, only to find themselves at the mercy of an angry white mob. According to the story, her father caught wind of the unfolding assault and raced home with a shotgun in hand. Throwing the car's gear shifter into park, he leaped out, ready to defend his home. A local police officer reportedly echoed old tropes, stating, "If you bust a cap, I'll let them do what they want."

On that day, Opal's family home was destroyed and burned to the ground simply because of the color of their skin. That day was Juneteenth—yes, on the very day intended to signify the end of slavery, their home and sense of safety were deeply violated.

Imagine stepping into my shoes for just a moment, or perhaps part of a day, in Dallas during the winter of 2025. Your mission is to share Opal's story in front of 1,500 people, many of whom admire her for her achievements. It was a distinct honor to share the stage with the woman who, through her unwavering commitment to honoring those who came before her, single-handedly orchestrated the declaration of Juneteenth as a national holiday. This assignment raised as many questions as it provided answers, even though this wasn't your first rodeo.

I'll take you out of the cockpit for a moment. The art of storytelling inspires me to focus on the organic narrative twists in our stage conversation and the paths we can explore. The science would keep us in the cockpit, prepared to follow set questions, thereby increasing our chances of success. I vividly recall that morning.

Wake up.

Work out.

Read. Read some more.

Watch interviews of Opal during her famous 2.5-mile walks, symbolizing the two-and-a-half years it took for the Emancipation Proclamation to reach Texas.

Rewatch them and brew another cup of hotel coffee while the HVAC hums on autopilot.

I mechanically meander through my preparations for our live event but struggle to find peace. Everything urges me to stick to what I know—reading the room and the guest beside me while I curiously explore topics and timeframes in history to extract their story.

I also realize I have one chance to get it right.

I need to acknowledge her age and treat her with great respect. I enjoy a good film score to stimulate my creativity, but this task feels different. I can't simply paraglide over the mountains of expected outcomes to do her story justice—this must be artful.

As I sifted through outfit options, I finally found a soft landing for the herky-jerky track I had embarked on:

I should focus on the hidden stories, experiences, and rarely documented moments shared in her substantial biography.

I thought that if the audience wished, they could read or watch highlights of Opal's accomplishments over the decades. I won't bore you with every question I asked, but I will share that my first query was about her mother's kitchen, while the last one concerned a near-miss story that revealed more about Opal's motivations than her methods or achievements.

After providing brief remarks on the power of storytelling, I escorted Opal onto the stage and into the high-back chairs pre-set for our discussion. The bright lights dimmed as an introductory video of Opal's life and accomplishments began to play. A powerful montage of nationwide walks and White House visits teed up my initial question to Opal as the energy in the room continued to build for this cultural icon. "Opal, take me inside your mother's kitchen. What did it smell like?" I knew I got the proverbial bat on the ball when she rolled all of us into an, "… oooohhhhhhh" as only a grandmother could emote. Sure, there were sound bites to capture about civil rights, burning buildings, and race relations, but we needed to create ambiance for the event.

It was immediately clear that Opal, despite her current age and being in her 99th year on this planet, had the burning fire of life at the ready.

In 1959, Opal was already a genuine firecracker of a woman. A teacher, an advocate, a mother—the list goes on. She was about to meet Martin Luther King Jr. for the first time on the campus of what was then Brite College, now part of Texas Christian University (TCU). The only visit King would make to Fort Worth was arranged by Dr. Vada Felder, the first African American to graduate from Brite.

Felder passed away in 2008 at the age of 97. Although I never had the opportunity to meet her, I can only assume her light shone as brightly as the radiance emanating from Opal's smile when she told our audience that she was *everyone's grand-mother* to open our dialogue that day in Dallas.

Opal unfortunately did not attend Felder's event at the Majestic Theater, where 400 community members gathered for Dr. King's sermon, "A Great Time to Be Alive." Rather than walking through the front doors of the Majestic as a Black woman, experiencing an entryway that had previously been forbidden to her for the first time, she chose to be at a local hospital for the birth of her friend's first child.

Rewind to the luncheon just before our shared keynote on stage in Dallas—a moment for me to share a meal with Opal, foster chemistry, and ease any nerves she might have. Despite all the handwringing I did in room 2387, I never considered her connection to Martin Luther King Jr. I researched her achievements, her family, her letter to President Barack Obama, and her children's book. Yet, as we sat down, pretending not to notice the growing gallery of onlookers, it occurred to me to ask her about King.

We were discussing my children when I recalled my conversation with my daughter about *who* should complete her vocabulary homework. I had been so focused on the details that I thought the audience wanted to hear that I overlooked the fact that the best stories come from curiosity—the kind that artfully fuels young children's imaginations.

This time, I would do my darndest to meet the moment, even with the heat of stage lights barreling across my brow. I knew our time on stage was about to end when I asked her to share the story of King, not for name recognition, but for the message her story represented about the value a single tree lends to the forest canopy.

Opal's previous "ooohhh" was returned by the audience as a collective, "… ahhh" when hearing how she chose her friend over Martin Luther King Jr.

The audience got it!

I had been so focused on the answer I thought they were seeking from the interview that I almost missed a golden opportunity to tag them into the human side of Opal's life. That day, I felt like part of the audience filled with amazement at the moments captured, celebrated, and advocated for by the enduring flame of Opal Lee.

Meeting the moment often requires us to embrace narratives that are greater than ourselves to truly appreciate the power of story within each of us.

★ ★ ★

One could argue that we are generally conditioned to seek answers, share them widely, and hold onto them indefinitely. I recall a time when political sentiment favored leaders who adjusted their views as new information emerged. We valued political pivots resulting from fresh insights.

It seems increasingly evident today that answers and subsequent proclamations operate like self-locking systems, never to be challenged for fear of being labeled weak. The irony is that we teach our children to develop ideas and thoughts that evolve into hypotheses, which are tested, twisted, contorted, and shaped from one side of a data set to another before even considering a conclusion.

Within this paradox lies the art and science of storytelling—stories provide endings, even if only temporary. The fluid nature of our imagination transforms one-hit wonders into timeless trilogies and single events into annual celebrations. Stories can conclude at any moment, and even some of the most critically acclaimed films fail to meet our expectations for a natural ending. Relationships can end before they even begin. Job openings today may close before dusk, and quotes for a car loan can expire at the worst possible times.

The inverse, however, is that stories can evolve postmortem into epilogues and final tour stops, shifting from previews to smash hits. Repeated storylines that we struggle to escape in our personal and professional relationships tug at our need to be wanted by the characters who define our life experiences.

> The **art of storytelling** involves recognizing clear patterns among the elements unique to each story.
>
> The **science of storytelling** involves crafting fundamental patterns into new sequences that resonate with the present moment and reflect our intentions and presence without bias against misgivings, others, or ourselves.

To genuinely engage with the moments that shape our lives, we should reflect on the following questions as part of a healthy balance between the art and science of representing ourselves through storytelling.

1. How can stepping back to view the "forest" alter your perspective on the individual "trees" both at home and at work that represent your story?
2. What criteria should you use to determine which stories are most meaningful to share and why?
3. How might finding the core narrative in your experiences transform your sense of purpose?

Professional Moments

In my view, writing a book is somewhat similar to a series of public revelations about ourselves—not about others or events—but about the good, the indescribable, the slightly off-kilter, the mildly scandalous, and, most notably, the embarrassing. Taking a stand at a fixed point in one's life to communicate lessons requires aggressively smashing plastic from innocent palms, Hungry Hippos–style, to remember and collect as many lessons, or marbles, as possible in order to piece together the meaning of the last few decades.

That's it.

We should not complicate matters, even if it sounds better. A classic game for toddlers about control and possession serves as a fitting metaphor for our primal instinct to survive and ultimately win.

When we lack a North Star to pursue, our legs wobble. Purpose can be a powerful elixir for the vastness of human experience. This is exactly why incentive structures are established at all levels of life to spark a shift from yesterday's malaise to tomorrow's pursuit.

Sales professionals eagerly adopt incentive structures through rigorous, artificial peer competition. Entrepreneurs pursuing investment strategically manipulate timing to highlight the exclusive opportunity to chase their unique professional dreams. Uncovering the narrative within ourselves requires reflective moments that are challenging to develop without the influence of others. Situations shaped by others offer us chances to respond, thrive, or falter.

Regardless of your employment status or the industry you represent, an entrepreneurial mindset thrives across cultures. The following questions aim to clear the murky windshield of stories seeking sunlight and exposure to connect the past, present, and future. This internal dialogue surrounding the questions reshapes the narrative of your life into stanzas of possibility for tomorrow.

Be honest with yourself.

I'll join in, too!

The first question encompasses the entire process of securing a position, leading a departmental meeting, branching out, and crafting your script as an entrepreneur. We are often motivated by a desire to distinguish ourselves from our peers for all the right reasons.

How have I conveyed my achievements to my colleagues?

What is the narrative arc of my achievements?

A common misconception among early-career professionals arises during the interview process: the success of a single story transforms a candidate into a professional storyteller. In the initial interview, job seekers regard one or two stories as their proverbial go-tos.

It works. A second interview is scheduled.

Then, for some reason, the candidate believes they need to create new stories to share as they progress through the interview process. As this typical scenario unfolds, the stories lose their impact, resulting in questions from higher-ups about what was initially perceived as intriguing in the candidate.

Entrepreneurs feel this urge whenever they seek investment or present their product or solution to a potential customer.

What case studies can I share?

Which case stories should I share?

The science of storytelling suggests examining patterns of similarity between your prospective client's or investor's and past customer stories. The art of storytelling will guide you like a lazy river down a less-traveled path to discover the unique connections you and your company may share with the prospect. Artistry emerges as you highlight the elements of connection and understanding through lessons learned and shared experiences.

Without ceremony, I can say that I presented in front of investors—a moment of "I can't believe I just did that," which, in hindsight, revealed my lack of understanding of the game being played. I couldn't see the forest for the trees, often overly focused on our vision for the future, the landscape we would create together, and the successes we would achieve.

Successful entrepreneurs, along with some charlatans, advised me to focus on the process. This meant I should discuss our thought processes, highlight the strength of the team's achievements, and outline the framework for a working relationship—not just for the anticipated good times but also for the lean moments when resumes are as valuable as the paper they are printed on.

The gig economy seems to be a constant presence for everyone, and one essential aspect of success is the narratives we share, highlighting the depth of our accomplishments while resonating with the aspirations of others seeking new horizons. We must confidently express our value while also illustrating significance through shared experiences, providing a glimpse into a world where we connect with others.

One of my favorite quotes may not be historically accurate or relevant, but it highlights the profound desire that humans, as social beings, have for stories that gain recognition:

The only battle I have ever fought against is insignificance.

Actress Jessica Chastain portrayed Catherine Weldon in *Woman Walks Ahead*. Set in the late 19th century, the film follows her journey to Dakota to paint Sitting Bull's portrait, where she becomes intertwined in the Lakota's struggle for sovereignty. Amid the clash of cultural norms and narratives, Weldon and Sitting Bull come to understand each other's motivations. Her poignant and heartfelt quote further emphasizes her goal of capturing Sitting Bull's story.

A canvas of less dramatic strokes often comes into focus during conference room or Zoom meetings, where peer pressure drives us into comparative storytelling about our weekends, significant sales calls, or strategies, with each round-robin more compelling than the last. You might call these micro-stories, but in truth, they are narratives we consciously create, layering conviction, emotion, defeat or denial, desperation or regret, and embellishments of a proposed Herculean feat.

Think about this: Is the purpose of the story you decide to share to evoke compassionate responses from others?

Are you intending to share stories to enhance the positive perception of your role and contributions?

Do you often choose stories that automatically portray you as either the hero or the victim? If so, what is the reason?

Vulnerability and honesty in sharing our stories create a platform for connection. Professionally, I felt a responsibility to the audience in Dallas to help convey Opal's story. Focusing on the obvious would only position me alongside every other storyteller or journalist who relied on simplistic narratives, earning lukewarm applause for the predictable.

You may not find yourself on stages or alongside historical figures, but this lesson is relevant for everyone. The art and science of storytelling emphasize individual skills and abilities that are pertinent and transferable across all levels of the professional ladder and landscape.

Our ability to discern nuance in others' talking points paves the way for your contributions and ideas to take flight.

You will be noticed.

You will increase opportunities.

Personal Moments

I can vividly remember the crushing experience of rejection in young love—not the kind we face as adults, but the one that hits us like a school locker before an exam. I wanted to find a song that would let me selectively drown in sorrow and what-if scenarios. The big picture often felt like a titanic zero to me. In that moment, my life was forever altered by the sudden end of my relationship. Forget seeing the forest; I wanted to fall from the tree to the unforgiving ground below.

I'll take a risk (a bit of narrative humor never hurt anyone) and assume you're familiar with the emotional threshold of pain I'm describing: the songs, the moments you spotted them with someone new, the anger, the outrage that your story was no longer cute, enticing, or, dare I say, valued.

Our connection to the delicate ecosystem of love and relationships runs deep beneath the surface of avatars and appealing Facebook posts. Pain and rejection often mark the end of one chapter and the beginning of another.

The reality of teenage heartache is that these emotional car crashes sharpen our discernment between fantasy and reality. It's a struggle between our desires and our necessities. For those of us who grew up in relatively resourceful and opportunistically (though not financially) affluent environments, the line between wants and needs often becomes blurred. Calluses accumulate over time, honing our ability to withstand disappointment while simultaneously leaping toward opportunity.

The questions I eagerly want to ask interviewees typically focus on their responses to disappointment rather than on their achievements. If I perform my job well, I can uncover their fundamental approach to navigating the world. Consider the following questions, observations, and probing inquiries to help frame where your *desires* should contrast with your *needs*:

- How do you view the journey of your relationship with love?
- Share a story about friendship that shows your hope for enduring connections and the sadness experienced when they diminish.
- Do your friendships enrich your story or take away from it?
- What do others perceive about the role you play in your friendships?

These elements aim to uncover the roles we play both in the moment and within a broader context. Can we remain authentic and honest when assessing our desires and the lengths to which we will go to construct this narrative?

Can we see the forest for the trees?

The Narrative Edge

It's fair to say that we are always seeking an edge in business, at home, on the ballfield, when we board a plane, request a window seat at a must-visit restaurant, negotiate real estate deals, or try to teach our children life lessons through the apparatus of homework.

It's perfectly acceptable to seek an advantage. The real question, however, is how we can transform our life experiences into meaningful stories that genuinely and accurately reflect our character, purpose, vulnerabilities, and aspirations to an audience of one or many.

The edge we seek, with varying degrees of intensity, helps us recognize the stories of those around us and their impact on the narratives we create about ourselves. I almost always ask two questions during an interview because I know I will receive a response that feels off-script and genuine.

- How would you define your relationship with success?
- What is your exit plan?

These two questions serve a couple of objectives:

1. The first question encourages us to reflect on how we have valued, defined, and experienced success over time. This question connects my internal and external voices, allowing me to explore the intersecting narratives that evaluate wants and needs.
2. The second question isn't actually about leaving something; it's primarily about recognizing the larger context surrounding your current situation. An exit plan seamlessly integrates with an entrepreneur's strategy and an investor's decision to participate or abstain. The exit plan in a relationship brings a sense of reality to its spirit and sentiment. Do you take pride in the struggle to achieve your goals, or do you linger in a world of what-ifs and regrets, often succumbing to paralyzing anxiety?

Seeing the forest for the trees can be gut-wrenchingly tricky, as it often seems that doing so signals a resolution is in sight. If we view a relationship from the broad perspective of an endless Nordic day and night of darkness, we may need to decide whether to continue or end a once-promising love. Conversely, we might feel pressured to commit too soon while personal doubt continues to inhabit our minds.

Our work lives are quite similar, and the consequences can be more tangible than just bruised egos and conciliatory actions stemming from conflicts at home. The narrative of our value at work can fluctuate, often failing to reach the desired intensity at the right moment. When we seek the spotlight, it eludes us for others, and when we prefer to sink into our chairs, our voices and expertise emerge to the forefront.

A damned if you do, damned if you don't tug-of-war weaves an unlikely tapestry of opportunity for us all to sharpen our narrative edge. For a moment, consider this question:

Am I okay with not knowing the answer?

Yunus's AI work, alongside that of technologists worldwide, presents a somewhat forced choice: by providing answers to the challenges and obstacles of being human, must we shift our focus from addressing the question of *how* to construct inquiries about *why*? Yunus and I are exploring the possibility of interviewing deceased historical figures—a daunting yet thrilling proposition that places me squarely between artfully respecting lives well lived and meeting the knowledge appetites of today.

I hope the edge at which we live and die signifies something that Yunus's letter from ChatGPT to humans highlights: our uniquely human ability to articulate moments that connect the physical and emotional realms, offering us significant opportunities not just to survive but to thrive in a world where stories unfold independently, solutions arise with scientific precision, and the mystery only deepens across digital horizons and environments.

The story of Dr. King's singular visit to Fort Worth is not primarily about the sermon he delivered, but rather about Dr. Felder's unwavering determination. This occurred against the backdrop of common sense during a period of significant upheaval, as she sought to invite, host, and create a meaningful experience for local African Americans. One night in October 1959, they stepped through the Majestic Theater's front doors as equal citizens alongside those who chose not to attend. Opal, similarly, cast a shadow rich with intent during times of dissent.

Opal's success story isn't just about walking to Washington, D.C., or persuading the government to acknowledge a day of great celebration, complexity, and reflection; instead, it highlights a broader perspective. A woman celebrated for her advocacy and her wish to be everyone's grandmother exemplifies determination, even as the winds of deceit and denial swept across the nation. In a public letter, Opal reached out to President Obama, seeking his support.

The letter's closing clearly and succinctly illustrates the story of a strong oak tree among the wilted.

There are several other things I want to talk with you about. Here's hoping I can have an audience with you when I get there this winter. I'm looking forward to seeing you again.

Sincerely,
Opal Lee
Juneteenth Chair

P.S. You could save me a lot of shoe leather and a lot of wear and tear on an old body by saying how soon you can see me so I can get all my ducks in a row (all my questions) and not waste your time.

As I closed the door to room 2387 and headed down to Opal, I remembered thinking, "Let the art of her story shine without exposing the scientific stitching of storytelling to the audience." The art of storytelling feels organic when we recognize the science of the patterns that form around and through the tales that shape our lives.

Caretaker needed. Humanity calling. Ring tone ...

11 | Eulogizing Stories

The Sound Bites That Memorialize Your Story

Calligrapher available. Have pen. Need ink.

"In the moment." This is a common phrase used to capture the experience of being human. But what does it truly mean to be in the moment, and can we recognize when it is happening in real time? For me, this often-used phrase signifies being present without awareness of distinctions that lead to distraction. There are times in our lives that demand we present ourselves as fully aware of the gravity of the moment, the stillness of the moment, and the anticipation of the moment to come.

If only life worked in such a neat and tidy way.

If life were so prescriptive, we'd be able to plan for the moments that punctuate our storyline and most likely come out on whatever top signifies for that individual. This would rob us of critically important experiences that allow us to layer past

encounters with one another, producing compelling and immediate responses to the euphoria, tragedy, and wonders of living.

Saying "I do" in marriage or "I accept" a professional opportunity creates an immediate and powerful memory, emphasized
by our ability to be present and to experience a range of emotions equal to or greater than those words. If we can ride the
wave of being present, we increase our chances of meeting the
moment with words that truly match it.

Sometimes, we need to steer those we care about most away
from dark and unapologetic paths during the moments of life
that challenge all of us the most.

These are the moments when the respite we seek resides in
the stories we create, symbolizing and celebrating the experiences of others.

Uncle Rod ...

*Ashley, while we were a part of each other's lives for more than a decade,
I can't help but feel that our time together was far too short. I remember
your thoughtful words when I entered your family and married your
sister. I find solace in that a little bit of you is within Christie and beams
through your sweet children.*

*I would like to share a few words, as Uncle Rod, if I may ...
Dear Lilly, Gage, and Caden
Life is precious and ultimately written as a book of adventure, challenge,
and celebration. Each turn of the page invites feelings of wonder and
excitement—sometimes fear and sometimes sadness. I wish I had an
answer for you about the "why" we are here today and why your book
reads as it does today.*

*What I can share with you is that your mother was human in every
sense of the word—perfect and imperfect, sweet and, like your aunt, a
little sassy, loving, and sometimes distant.*

Your bond with your mother extends beyond what we know here on Earth. Your days may be filled with questions, confusion, happy thoughts and memories, bouts of anger and frustration for the incompleteness of your time here on Earth with her.

Ashley, you created three uniquely loving, talented souls who will eventually find solace in the love and support of your friends and family here today. My wish for you, Ashley, is that you secure your front-row seat to the sweet moments Lilly, Gage, and Caden will experience and share together, the times they overcome insurmountable odds and achieve their dreams.

Ashley, may you dance with Lilly in her dreams.
May you wrestle and bound playfully through Gage's mind and sweet curls
May you whisper to Caden when he feels alone, when he dreams of his momma and explores love that began with you, and lights up and through Morgan

Ashley, may you find a mirror in heaven just for you
  May you see yourself as we, here on Earth, see you
    May you peer beyond your glance to see all of us
      blowing you a sweet kiss from below

While we mourn your loss, please know that you left an indelible mark on all of us. While you may not be with us in body, we feel you in spirit.

Through sudden and gentle breezes … through spectacular sunsets and puffy clouds
… you are loved and forever in our hearts

Sincerely and with love,
Uncle Rod

★ ★ ★

It was spring 2020, and the world we knew was disintegrating. Like many others, I wanted to reach out to friends to see how they were managing, connect, and discuss the pandemic, yet I refrained. It felt like slowly driving past a car accident on the freeway. News reports seemed more dire with each passing day, and the enemy remained invisible. Honestly, I hadn't felt this way since the days immediately following 9/11. At that time, I was living in Los Angeles, and I remember the unverified reports that terrorists were threatening our water supply and that more chaos was about to descend upon the U.S.—a complete and utter nightmare for the nation.

On a fairly typical spring day at the start of the pandemic, I connected once again via Zoom with Richard Gerver, the award-winning educator and well-known TED speaker, who would surely have the words to describe the pandemic's impact.

Richard's rugby-like silhouette always gave way to a teddy bear face that was constantly responsive to my ramblings. We joked around, sharing nods that reflected our fear for our families and communities. Then we heard it …

"NOOOOOOOOOOO!!!!!"

I asked Richard for a moment to find out what my wife was screaming about. This wasn't a "spilled milk" scream; it was a guttural sound echoing through the house. Bouncing off the walls as I hurried around corners and down the hallway, I found my wife sobbing. Her younger sister, still in her early 30s and a mother of three, had passed away.

I didn't have any answers, nor did I possess a playbook for supporting my wife. I was the guy with the stories, essentially a man left with a piece of paper and no pen. I repeated my frantic sliding across the floor, crashing into walls as I tried to reach Richard. What could he be thinking? He must have heard her scream. I cobbled together a mishmash of words to convey the news of my sister-in-law's death. Richard expressed his love for us, and then the Zoom call disconnected.

We don't know how, why, or even when stories take unexpected turns, but that is the power of life. That morning, I believed the only challenge I faced was the pandemic. I would have never imagined that I would also confront the death of a loved one, surrounded by more questions than answers.

I opened this chapter with the eulogy I delivered at my sister-in-law's graveside funeral. The family asked if I would consider eulogizing Ashley. I was the storyteller, the one who loved words—or so it was pitched to me.

The lesson isn't that we need to become proficient in storytelling to eulogize our loved ones; rather, it lies in our ability to understand the characters and scenes that compose a person's life. Story, for all of us, finds its place in these corners of life, offering us opportunities to eulogize, report, write, preach, observe, and participate in ways that suit the circumstances and our role in the larger narrative.

The day of the funeral felt like a Christopher Nolan film noir, emphasizing the black, gray, and white of the visual canvas. The graveside service was painted with a broad and unforgiving brush, swirling clouds heading toward an apex of crackling. The warm air struggled to reach me beneath the strangled bundle of nerves tightening my top button and necktie. There was nowhere to hide. Three sets of eyes darted between Uncle Rod and the bows and laces constricting their feet. I only hope that my version of their mother's impactful story captured the essence of her being for those carrying on her smile.

A eulogy, as a form of storytelling, compels you to reflect on others. To write a eulogy with compassion and significance, you must consider each person affected by the loved one who has passed away.

A few short months after the funeral, I found myself in the unenviable position of having to leave the company I built because a fraudster had boxed me out. As I spoke with my attorney about how to proceed, it was clear that I would need to craft a story in the form of a resignation letter. Much like the eulogy given just months earlier, I had to consider all the characters, both good and bad, who played a part in this chapter of my life. In short, I had to eulogize my presence. To this day, it remains one of the more unusual storytelling assignments I've embarked upon.

★ ★ ★

It was the 1980s, as one of my favorite shows always begins (*The Goldbergs* on ABC), and I was an awkward teenager trying to find my place in school. Some days I could play the jock because I was on the middle school basketball team, while other days I could loosely fit into one of the more artsy groups, like choir, band, or theater. I'd like to think I was a thoughtfully curated music collection rather than just a wandering teenager.

One afternoon, leaving gym class, I found myself walking down the corridor from the gym, past the cafeteria on my way to my locker. I was walking with a few jocks, and a classmate named Tim (changed for the purposes of this book) was just a few steps ahead. Timmy, as he was called, struggled to fit in. He was above average in height and possibly below-average in being average. We never really knew if he had formal struggles socially or academically, but he was labeled as different.

Timmy had never done anything to me. He had never mocked me or really participated in any activity. He knew who I was, and I knew who he was. For some uncharacteristic reason, I felt that my story, that random day after gym class, needed a boost at Timmy's expense. The other boys I was casually walking with started teasing Timmy. Nothing physical, but definitely cringe-worthy. I remember it like it was yesterday—I decided to join in. I chirped at Timmy like I was the heartless party in a hit-and-run accident.

I suppose you could say that I felt whatever good feeling I could as we walked past the cafeteria. Later that night, it was a different story. I remember the overwhelming shame I felt.

I was Timmy.

I wasn't any different.

I fit into whatever normal was during those days, but I was fundamentally just like Timmy. I couldn't sleep, and after breakfast, all I could think about was getting to school.

Did he notice what I said, or was it drowned out by his own coping mechanism? I had no idea, but I knew I couldn't ignore what I had done.

Tim was gracious as I struggled to find the words to express how sorry I was for my actions. I learned that day about the power of narrative—the sound bites we put together tell a story about all of us. It was clear that my epiphany and apology would only resonate between Tim and me. I foolishly hoped it might impact the universe of mean-spirited teens who relentlessly tormented Timmy. I haven't seen or heard of Tim since the 1980s; I can only hope he found solace in stories of compassion and connection, realizing he was never who those cruel teens made him out to be.

There is a piece of Timmy in all of us.

Memories

One of the most powerful storytelling tools we possess in endless supply is our memories. They form a vast pool of rich colors and textures, fueled by the sounds of the moment, the songs in our hearts, and the vibrations of the many firsts we experience as humans. Memories are wrapped in emotions, cementing their place in our psyche until the very end.

The challenge and opportunity for our storytelling abilities hover over the chance to click on memories, free from bias, allowing us to relive moments that capture our experiences. We dive into these stories when we have a single opportunity to connect with an audience. This is why we often discuss our children or family life at the beginning of any significant speech—because we want to tap into a fundamental human experience that, statistically speaking, others in the audience can relate to.

I remember learning about dreams and their timing in recirculating in patients' minds the night before a session when I was in professional mental health practice. You might even say there is a certain level of permission structure associated with our dreams that allows them to come out when the coast is clear or when we are in the presence of acceptance from another.

Memories remind us of the untold story, the suppressed story, and the narrative that longs to be shared.

A few years ago, I worked behind the scenes with Formula 1 and the Williams Racing team in Austin, Texas. I interviewed their current top driver, Alex Albon. Despite Alex being a young professional athlete, I recall feeling like I was sitting with a son—not my own, but he had a certain sensibility about him. The stories he shared weren't just about conquests on the track. Alex came alive when he talked about a homemade figure-eight track his father had built when he was a boy. The land wasn't theirs, and his father had to get permission to create it, but it felt like it belonged to them. Round and round, Alex studied each curve and how his vehicle responded. It's a memory and a story that likely stays with him now as a famous Formula 1 driver.

Fast-forward, and I began receiving interview requests from authors and their publicists because word on the street was that I would get to the heart of their memoirs, especially those from days gone by. One particular memoir was a collection of memories linked to dire and generational consequences. Linda Ambrus Broenniman's book, *The Politzer Saga,* reminded me of the power of memories in the stories we share. I found Linda to be a kind soul and almost an apologetic interview guest, showing great respect for the process and for those she truly represented in her powerful portrayal.

A house fire claimed her mother's life, uncovering a hidden box of documents and photographs. Linda had grown up as a Catholic, unaware until the accident that her family was concealing the secrets of eight generations of Jewish ancestors in Hungary. Her captivating retelling transported me through World War II Europe, revealing both devastation and hope through characters who had been there all along. Clara Ambrus, Linda's mother, sheltered Jews during the war, later receiving recognition at Yad Vashem in Israel as "Righteous Among the Nations," alongside Oscar Schindler and others. For Linda, memories had taken on a new shape and a different place in her heart and mind, impacting all of us fortunate enough to hear her story.

I hope to visit the permanent exhibition of the boxed findings at the Rumbach Synagogue in Budapest one day.

A collection of memories eulogized for us to learn from and live by as storytellers and global citizens.

Professional Moments

Do you have friends who fear certainty? Friends or even colleagues who muddle along the fringes out of fear that any declaration, one way or the other, will cause more harm than living a life of, "whatever you think …" There is something striking about the finality of a resignation or a funeral service—a distinct moment in time when others look to us to meet the moment.

For many of us, there are breadcrumbs along the way that hint at a world filled with decisions just waiting to be made. Whether it's which sport to focus on, the day you declare your major in college, or the moment you say yes to a job offer, a marriage proposal, or a cohabitation arrangement.

Pivotal moments happen every second of every day, and with each passing moment comes the chance to commemorate the achievement through a story. This is a common challenge for leaders of businesses of all types and sizes:

- How can we celebrate our wins?
- What are the implications of celebrating others for their contributions to the collective?
- Are we overvaluing or undervaluing the team's accomplishments?

One of my favorite shows of all time is *Seinfeld*. I still watch clips and old episodes, laughing at the same jokes and anticipating the ones to come. A classic episode pits Elaine (Julia Louis-Dreyfus) against her boss and cultural icon J. Peterman (John O'Hurley) over how often the office celebrates employee birthdays, anniversaries, and the like. Elaine nearly dry heaves at the thought of another birthday song echoing through the air ducts of the J. Peterman Company.

You might think this is funny and trite. But did you know that companies, especially startups, have taken Elaine's complaint, buried it deep, and doubled down on employee engagement initiatives masked as celebrations?

The question for well-intentioned, quality leaders is how to enable authentic storytelling that resonates, avoids becoming white noise, and fosters a culture of awareness and impact to withstand future and, most likely, inevitable change.

Personal Moments

The idea of a take-back or a mulligan brings out the youthful side of me, and I'd wager it does for some of you as well. We lived whimsical lives where consequences were merely things we read about or saw on television shows or in movies. One of the wonders of storytelling is the ability to cash in a take-back or ask for a mulligan when life veers off the expected path.

I was living in Los Angeles—or should I say, lost in Los Angeles. I wasn't sure if I was living the life I had dreamed of or desperately seeking refuge in the stories of others. I hung around actors and wannabes, and if I'm honest, I could have been a member of any or all of these groups rummaging through the City of Angels. One Friday night, I met a woman who was quite unlike the masses I had encountered during my first two years of hard knocks in L.A. She was a designer. She was measured, literally.

Measure twice.

Cut once.

I found the rigid and very professional behavior inviting. I was desperately seeking relief from the smog of indecision and star-crossed nights. Fast-forward a few months, and shared trips to the grocery store turned into two sets of toothbrushes, and one day I found myself engaged to be married. Even now, I can't say that I was authoring the story when it felt like I was within a story—a subtle but distinct difference, like a note in a glass of wine you think you've experienced before but aren't quite sure.

I'll spare you and her the spilling of marital beans. I will, however, note that while this should have been a time in my life memorialized by the beauty of storytelling, it wasn't. I never felt comfortable in the role I was asked to play or the one I allowed myself to play. There was no malice, on either side, to assign. We thought we were authoring a shared manuscript, only to discover creative differences in the protagonist that splintered any chance of longevity.

The second time around, I wanted something different. I aimed to think boldly about the choice I was making and the one she would be making by saying yes. The closing of my proposal to my now-wife and the mother of my children was a story presented in video form. I didn't want to look back one day and wonder how the proposal was conceived. This isn't to say there is just one way to capture the personal moments that mark a life well-lived.

The flip side of the well-orchestrated proposals of business or marriage lies waiting on the fringes of events we turn our backs on. For me, it was missing the graduation ceremonies. I'll admit it's a bit odd to consciously choose to miss your own graduation ceremony. A guy in the cheap seats at a minor league baseball game might chime in, suggesting that I didn't want to think about the endings to the stories I had constructed. Maybe, after a couple of dollar beers, he'd extend the conversation by openly contemplating my need to have an opening to leave, to rewrite, to call a take-back, or to cancel a subscription to a belief, a relationship, or a career path.

I'd probably buy that guy a beer.

If I had known what I know now after inquiring about so many memorializing moments created by iconic figures in innovation, fame, fortune, and professional success, I might ask my younger self questions to understand my role in the outcomes I experienced.

I would ask myself:

- How do you perceive finality?
- When you lie down at night, do you reflect on your choices through a lens of regret or pride, considering those that resemble life's most important decisions?

Narrative Edge

There is a fine line between the nobility associated with contribution and the martyrdom of sympathy-seeking storytellers. The narrative edge we aim to convey at home and in our professional pursuits carries with it the sultry siren of compassion, enticing us to surrender to the softer side of life. If we are not careful, our stories might start to sound like skipping vinyl on a retro record player. If every story we told ended in triumph, we would be no better than the schools and athletic teams that hand out honorable mentions. Life and the stories that chronicle its wonders do not necessarily need to be Hollywood grand; rather, the relative impact of a story on and through each of us is what truly matters.

If I didn't know any better, I might land on this planet wondering why there are so many victims of life, circumstance, and the bumps and bruises that come with the natural course of living. This isn't about actual victims of crime but rather those who, in order to maintain the role they feel most comfortable in, act in ways and share stories that inevitably seek consolation from others.

Finding our narrative edge encourages us all to be our own audience in the one-person show that is our life. The challenging stories, the tales of joy, and the narratives that illustrate a life well-lived urge us to ask probing questions—not to dismiss them but to clarify our role and the approach taken to propose a narrative we can support. In films, I'm always amazed by time-lapsed moments accompanied by emotionally moving music. The grandeur of epic climaxes in cinema hints at a successful journey across familiar storylines from despair to wonder. Over a few hours on a Saturday afternoon, we can experience a decade's worth of pain, suffering, enlightenment, and acceptance through movie magic.

While we might wish our current circumstances away with the same flair as a Hollywood montage, we should consider hunkering down—chronicling the experiences and feelings of challenging and inspiring situations at home, work, and within our communities in the form of a story. A basic but essential component in the development of our narrative edge lies in activation—activating an active rather than passive, time-lapse approach to the story that is our daily existence. Activating our stories in pursuit of our narrative edge means we must forge ahead, answering questions that bridge time, space, and moments together in an honest reflection of our legacy and the memories representing intention.

The following list of questions is overarching on purpose because it forces each of us to think about the footprints we create in the context of the world around us, indicating the direction ahead and where we came from.

- What stories do you hope others will share about you once you're gone?
- How well does your current narrative align with the legacy you wish to leave?

- What core values do your most significant stories convey?
- How can living with your legacy in mind change your daily storytelling?

As I exchanged wedding vows with my wife Christie on a warm day in mid-September 2010, I felt the laces of my shoes loosen and the collar of my shirt tighten as she gazed into my eyes, unscripted, and said, "… you matter." Those two little words are inscribed on the inner bands of my wedding ring— words that comfort me in times of confusion and emotional need. They became especially pivotal when I was tasked with eulogizing my sister-in-law.

We all matter. Our stories persist on Earth and beyond through recollections, memories, and narrative experiences infused with the humanity we showed others in their time of need. We can tell stories, or we can choose to be part of stories.

The decision lies with us.

Problem? Free advice. Name your price.

12

Life on the Big Screen

Your Story—Your Opus

The best is now, for now.

I don't know about you, but I have always been the kid and adult mesmerized by the transcendent experience of movies. I vividly remember being taken to see *Return of the Jedi* (1983) because it was the first time I sat in the front row. The intensity of the sound as George Lucas's story unfolded before my six-year-old eyes was mind-blowing. More popcorn slipped through my buttery fingers than I actually ate while I consumed the grandeur of the epic film.

About a year later, I had the opposite experience: I asked to leave the then-scary movie *Gremlins*. To this day, I am perfectly fine with passing on the cult hit, which featured cute, cuddly creatures turning evil through the gross and shocking scenes of the mid-'80s.

I must also admit that *Good Will Hunting*, starring Matt Damon and Ben Affleck, helped guide me through the long walks across the campus of Michigan State University. Some showings inspired me, some met me when I was angry and vengeful, and at other times, I saw the coming-of-age tale as an emotional, comforting story as I, too, wrestled with what to do—a relatively normal college experience but nonetheless, a maddening self-exploration into the path ahead, forged or not, that many of us have to take.

The eight times I purchased a *Hunting* ticket, I was making a down payment on understanding myself, even if only incrementally more than the day before. I was searching for a narrative to help me grasp my own story. This is why songs resonate with us, art captivates us, and the scent of a candle soothes us.

As you reflect on the authenticity of your story and your role in it, I suggest emphasizing its what-ifs and buts.

Sounds a bit harsh. One reason we fall in love with the stories of others is the experience of pausing our own narrative, for better or worse, and allowing another story to overlay our own. Think of it as beta-testing a different life without having to swap out your children for those down the street or a struggling job for one filled with control, responsibility, and necessary income.

We love second-chance stories because we hope to get a second chance if and when we need to cash in. We can see ourselves as villains alongside those we watch seeking retribution or vengeance. We can also picture ourselves as heroes in our dreams when we struggle to find courage when it's least expected of us in real life.

Once we become comfortable with our story, how it has unfolded, and the forecast for how it might develop, we have a distinctly human opportunity to share it with those we cherish the most. Great stories and storytellers seldom provide clear answers or explicitly reveal the intentions of the hero or villain. At times, stories powerfully address the character's predicament, and we embrace the narrative because we are actively seeking tales that resonate with our current state of mind or our desire for something new.

Mr. Destiny, starring Jim Belushi, Michael Caine, Linda Hamilton, and Courteney Cox (1990), spins a classic tale of "What if" through a middle-aged married man pondering what might have happened if he had hit the hanging curveball instead of striking out all those years ago. Critical acclaim likely evaded the cast and crew of *Mr. Destiny*. Nevertheless, the narrative effectively illustrates our inherent desire to consider different outcomes and our role in those conclusions. Self-determination, by lofty standards, offers all of us the at-bat we strive for—leaving it up to us whether or not we swing.

I've been stupid-lucky throughout life, closing my eyes at night only to open them to horizon lines I could have only imagined through National Geographic or the movies. Despite all the jet lag and bursts of excitement, I've always wanted opportunities to take my swings. Only while writing *The Narrative Edge* did I realize that Belushi's alternative ending might have inspired a storytelling approach in me. It's a friendly reminder that I can only expand my skill set or the horizons I gaze upon if I step into the batter's box as much as I can.

Sometimes, the story I think I'm capturing misses the point or undermines the narrative. Occasionally, the sound of my first step across a stage reverberates hollowly in an empty theater. It has taken me a few decades, but I finally realize that the audience I should be writing for isn't in front of me; it's inside me.

The impact we hope to have on those around us can only be fully realized if the audience inside us supports our effort to represent ourselves authentically.

I recall a high school relationship that fundamentally changed me and, dare I say, set my sails full of wind for the journey I know as my life. I was in what I still believe to be one of the most challenging years of high school—sophomore year. This period was tough because the excuse of freshman woes only faintly lingered while the weight of junior and senior years felt like summits I'd prefer not to tackle. During this time of acne, gangly arms, and subtle stashes, I met a fellow student who was unlike anyone I usually interacted with. You know the type— the judges, the know-it-alls, the jocks, and the ones whose parents have deeper pockets than yours, and so on. It felt like the high school equivalent of a dark comedy where a new social nightmare could become real every day.

Tony was different by every measure. He could not walk and relied on a motorized cart and a staff member who acted as his educational concierge. I think of Tony occasionally because he always jolted me out of the story I wanted to sulk into, like a turtle recoiling into its shell. Tony's smile was a mile wide and an ocean deep, often pulling me from the depths of what felt like a rough life into a world of optimism, laughter, and hope. He suffered from cerebral palsy, and I found myself sitting with him for lunch on Tuesdays. Those Tuesdays weren't like Mitch Albom's award-winning book turned movie, *Tuesdays with Morrie* (1997), but in a moment of blurring my eyes to make the landscapes match, they do. Albom's chronicling of time spent with Morrie was as much about the impact Mitch had on Morrie as it was about the impact Morrie had on Mitch.

Unbeknownst to Tony, those lunches were much more than breaking bread under the fluorescent lights of a busy school cafeteria. I was compelled to listen. I was compelled to observe and absorb. I was compelled to walk vulnerably with a boy whose perspective on life turned out to be a kaleidoscope of interests.

The lunches eventually transformed into visits to his home. I remember the first time I saw Tony glide across the floor with ease, no longer using a motorized scooter, ushering me into his version of Disney World.

We headed down into the basement, where we discovered a wondrous and enchanting world of trains, perfectly suited for a real-life portrayal of my holiday favorite, *The Polar Express* (2004). Tony joyfully shared the intricacies of his train collection—the sound of trains racing along the electric tracks—a rhythm only a model train set can produce. Round and round they went. Each pass gave me a chance to participate in Tony's story, and to this day, I am so glad I did. Of course, there were days I felt sad for what I believed Tony had missed by living a life outside what I considered normal. There were days I couldn't stop laughing, only to be matched by the roar of Tony's laughter.

What I know is that Tony's story is impactful. I had never allowed myself to empathize with another person's story like I did with Tony's. I often think back to those lunches and occasional afternoons with Tony during my travels to distant lands.

Sadly, I haven't seen Tony in decades, but I sure hope he knows he has traveled around the world with me. He has reminded me to open my senses to worlds and people with vivid stories unlike my own. Tony taught me more than he'll ever know.

Sometimes, stories discover us when we aren't even seeking them. The question remains: will we be ready to engage?

Interview

You and I are nearing our destination. We've journeyed through the annals of personal histories and narratives that conclude with every known punctuation mark. You probably picked up this book because you've heard about storytelling as an active approach and concept for becoming a better student, coach, parent, entrepreneur, or leader.

At the outset, I failed to mention that proficiency in personal and professional designations requires a comprehensive understanding of *why* stories matter. They matter not only because we gain insight into ourselves but also because they help us interpret the world around us and those who enter our horizon.

As we have throughout the book, let's roll up our sleeves and explore questions that will help you identify your opus.

Success: When did you first experience success, and how did it feel?

I distinctly remember being about four years old at a field day filled with competitive games and ribbons. I vividly recall the Hot Wheels race (as we called it back in the early 1980s). These were the pedal-powered, three-wheeled vehicles driven by Velcro shoes, which made a toddler feel *big*—*especially* when feeling *big* is such a significant deal.

I can't explain why it mattered so much, but I remember giving that race everything I had. I flew into each corner, hoping to slip by another little-big person. I even recall possibly skirting the inside of the orange cone instead of going around it. Thank goodness instant replay wasn't a thing during the Reagan administration. That fall day, I won the coveted blue ribbon and felt a sense of success that extended beyond my home and against my competitors.

My response to this question doesn't focus on the role of competition in our lives or imply that winning is the only goal. Success means different things to different people. To understand the story of success, we need to reflect on our own journeys and, perhaps more importantly, on the roles we've taken on over a lifetime of pursuits in many forms.

For many of us, especially young adults, it is common to feel a sense of expectation from our peer groups. If we are the alpha, our colleagues or classmates often believe we will lead a collective effort. If being the alpha doesn't feel right, but being a core team member does, then you will likely place yourself in the role that others expect of you. This is exactly why it is important to reflect on the roles you have taken in the past to determine if they align with the role you want to embrace in the future.

Your answer to the question of success will help you understand your character's motivations and fears, providing you with ample opportunities to revise or refine your responses today and tomorrow. Reflect on the origins of your motivations for success and how those initial influences or experiences shaped your current perception of what success looks and feels like.

Forgiveness: Have you reconciled your past with your present circumstances?

It might seem that I've mistakenly posed a dreaded yes/no query. Quite the opposite—upon reflection, I've asked a question that should elicit a teeter-totter response. "Well, I've reconciled the challenges of my childhood for the betterment of my family as a father and husband, but I've struggled to get out of my own way at work." These are just examples, but you understand the essence. Many of the stories we both push to the far reaches of our memory and those we keep emotionally close teeter between acceptance and repression.

That. Is. The. Human. Experience.

Celebrating the world we have created for ourselves requires a balanced effort in the narrative we present to ourselves— perhaps not intended for public sharing or even for those we love, but for our own reflection. Perhaps we're right in the midst of our own second-chance story. Perhaps we are the main characters in a struggle between redemption and retribution. Either way, we must grasp the *what* to understand the *why* of the stories that shape our personal and professional lives.

I love asking this question to those who are supremely accomplished in terms of material success and titles, as it aligns honesty with perception and reality. We all have heroes or figures we look to for inspiration, guidance, and what I call *feel-goods*. This question urges us to acknowledge the human condition and illustrates that Hollywood endings are merely illusions. Life begins not when we win a Hot Wheels race but when we face unexpected losses.

The answer to this question, if there is one, is likely quite convoluted for me—more resembling the gauges on my car's dashboard than anything linear or straightforward. This has been an ongoing process for me for a couple of reasons:

1. I have learned to transform my struggles into valuable contributions that I apply to my work and interactions. I am imperfect, but observing the struggles and celebrations of other cultures around the world has enabled me to reflect on my shortcomings without losing control of my narrative.

2. For years, I struggled with the idea that I had to or was preordained (a lofty word) to play the same role regardless of the situation. This often caused me great strife because of what I feared and what I thought I could be and accomplish.

Role: How has the contrast between winning and losing influenced your personal and professional narratives? Do you feel a stronger connection to an underdog or hero mentality, and why?

Whether we like it or not, we live in a world that celebrates differences through the prospect of winning and losing. We earn a spot in an academic program or a place on a sports team. We may miss out on a promotion or investment, or we might come in second to another buyer for a home. Life has a humorous way of setting the stage for us to play our parts. How we respond shapes the narrative that follows and the story that is ultimately assigned to our role.

Our culture fundamentally enjoys rooting for the underdog in sports, business, and other fields. Overcoming challenges reveals character traits within us, about us, and in relation to others. We wouldn't be human if we played only one side of this coin. A work of any merit uses the essence of down-on-our-luck experiences to highlight the self-defined successes that embody the very best of each of us.

When I ask CEOs this question in front of their companies, audiences lean in just a bit more, moving closer to see the response. Our opus isn't or shouldn't be about achieving some form of perfection or the perception of it. Our individual opus reflects the experiences we've gathered to learn more about ourselves, including our limitations and talents, and how we respond to the world around us.

If you asked me this question, I think about how many times I've been metaphorically knocked down professionally only to discover a new path forward. When I lost my job at a local technology company, I remember the intense and immediate panic washing over me. I was raised to believe that success is measured by longevity, yet here I found myself in need of a reboot, or a moment to turn the page. I certainly embraced the underdog label when I needed self-motivation to start each day with optimism rather than dread. The hero in me would make incremental progress each time I signed a contract with a new client for my startup. Their signature on a contract I created lifted my spirits as if I had circled the orange cones decades ago. I didn't succumb to external challenges; I thrived despite them! Honestly, these experiences as a business owner were likely the first time I transformed struggles into value, not because I followed a predetermined path but because I started from scratch.

As you explore your opus and the elements you consider representative of that journey, remember to include the moments that reveal your humanity more than scenes of bravado. One of my favorite moments during an interview with a CEO or startup founder is when I uncover the metaphorical trapdoor to the press-release stories they have struggled to share with me. Not because I enjoy digging up dirt or exposing the wickets of truth beneath the sheen of accomplishments, but because it is at that exact moment that the stories begin to flow.

Years ago, I met a buttoned-up education company CEO who could have played herself in a TV movie about her life. She was *her*, as the cool kids say these days. I was an immediate fan of her work in education technology and wasn't surprised by the accolades that began to pile up in her office quickly.

The first time I interviewed her, it was for a podcast. I remember being amazed by her ability, reminiscent of a seasoned politician, to recall facts and figures about her company and industry as if she were Oz. She had complete command of her story. After that initial interview, I found it difficult to identify the thread, the throughline to her narrative, which typically helped me create a headline that captured the essence or spirit of my subject. I couldn't understand why. She had guided me through the steps she took to reach the pinnacle. Her numbers were etched in both our memories, and she was kind and courteous.

Her publicist started flooding me with emails and calls to find out when I might finish the podcast and the related article.

I was confused, and then it struck me like a sudden cold snap after an early spring of warmer-than-usual temperatures.

She was too perfect. She reminded me of the accounting students I had previously worked with—more focused on perfection than on embracing the stories of struggle. I completed my work out of professional obligation and then contacted the publicist. A bit sheepishly, I shared my struggles and mentioned that I would defer any future requests to capture a story featuring the CEO. I was pleasantly surprised by the publicist's acknowledgment of her own struggles with the CEO.

It has served as a reminder, to this day, that stories stick because they relate to the audience.

Grand opening. Seats available. Please … please

The opus that represents each of us requires a commitment to understanding the emotional states we experience, the motivations behind the roles we play, and the desire to be noticed as we share our stories. The longing to have or secure an audience is genuine and fundamentally human. The orange jerseys of life serve as a reminder to consciously and actively consider the following when we create stories that reflect authentic experiences.

- Loneliness
- Role-playing (the victim, the hero, the savior, the antagonist)
- Applause versus condolences
- Hostile audience
- Aloof audience
- No audience

Once settled, embrace the classic red pen—not as an enemy, but as an editorial assistant that keeps you honest, reflective, and aware of the …

- Role embellishment plays in the telling of our stories
- Outcomes and conclusions we live versus those we desire

★ ★ ★

The lingering scent of popcorn and candy wafts across my nose. My head subtly sways like the top of a Pez dispenser clinging to its base. The show has been enjoyable yet heavy, and I'm ready to head home. It's that time of night when time seems to come to a standstill, each tick of the second hand stacking up like scar tissue over stories you'd rather move on from.

I vividly remember attending Broadway and off-Broadway shows as a kid. The lights, seats, and decor framed the stage, which seemed five stories high. I recall sharing glances with other kids who wanted to squirm out of their dress clothes, those who loved playing adult for an evening, and those who couldn't care less.

I didn't know then what I know now. Those privileged experiences exposed me to an often-overlooked idea of peering into another's story to construct your own narrative. Music filled the stage each time a scene began, ushering in captivating and emotional moments of heartache and eventual triumph. Those shows that weren't musicals introduced me to the power of words and, perhaps more importantly, the significance of the order in which those words relate to one another.

I suppose it was my first date with words or a first-love experience. Witnessing dramatic plays and the tightly delivered lines that changed lives, foretold doom, inspired dream machines from dust, and took the entire theater on an emotional rollercoaster.

Experiences like these are both entertaining and informative as you and I continue to decipher the stories we find ourselves wrapped in and those we fear will define us, as well as those we hope reflect our idealized intentions. I purposefully waited until our final scene or chapter to share one last vital element so that we could better appreciate the worth of our stories and the value they carry in the world we aspire to explore—not every story needs to be told.

You may have turned the pages of this book, believing that my intention was to help recruit better storytellers who succeed in their professional pursuits or personal relationships that thrive through active sharing. I guess there's a writer or editor who would argue that it's never appropriate to tell your reader they are wrong or mistaken, but in this case, I choose to disregard tradition.

By most definitions, currency represents a system of money that we all commonly use. Our understanding of the currency we share in the stories that connect us, highlight our differences, and guide our new journeys together sometimes requires silence.

This book is a love story about the power of narratives in my life and in the lives of those I've had the privilege of interacting with while capturing their stories around the world. The balance lies in holding onto stories when others need or command a stage for their own narrative. Don't confuse this with silencing your voice. Instead, think of it as your internal auditing system that says, "Okay, maybe I can learn from their story."

I don't believe we want a civilization of storytellers drowning each other out and hurling one story after another at one another. Never forget that stories are life, and life involves engaging all of our senses through different sheets of life's music, telling tales that support the efforts of the past and the pursuits of the future.

This book aims to unveil the stories, whether shared or kept hidden in our minds, that define and explain our experiences throughout life. It's up to you and the situation to decide whether to share a particular story or save it for a rainy day. Great storytellers are, above all, exceptional listeners. Your opus will differ from mine, which is not only acceptable but essential. Fine-tuning our listening skills will lead to storytelling that resonates in the moment. Our Narrative Edge encircles us—not finite or linear, but full, bright, and continuous, representing the fluid nature of story in relation to the experience of life. Our stories will never be complete literary works—they will build upon, evolve from, and illuminate the wonders of the world around us.

Isn't that all we want from the stories that patch together a life of good intentions and goodwill?

There are plenty of stories that you and I would gladly punt to another decade or century if we could, but the simple notion of recognition indicates that we are improving at reading our own stories. Ultimately, it is our choice to share or keep them to ourselves. I like to think about those who flaunt their wealth and the highly accomplished professionals who never send a flare of look-at-me into the night sky.

Each has a story.

Each has a choice.

Choose stories that resonate in the moment—whether on a first date, during a round of job interviews, while teaching a child, or when motivating your team during a timeout. That's the magic of storytelling: fluid experiences brought to life through images, letters, words, scenes, and the canvases of our determination.

Take a bow.

Your story matters …

Yours in Narrative,

Rod

You matter. We matter. Stories matter.

Acknowledgments

The story of success is often littered with dirty laundry, forget-table moments, and what-ifs. And, like any savvy kid who quickly cleans their room before parental footsteps precede piercing door knocks, the finished products or achievements that define us rarely include the slip-ups that paved the way forward.

I first dared to imagine authorship as a teen, believing I could muster the courage or the intestinal martyrdom to accomplish such a feat. Fast-forward a couple of decades, and this is either an autopsy of my mind strewn about as a collection of letters and words or an intermission of life events representing the people who have captured my attention and bottled it into meaningful, shared experiences.

I've loved and lost. I've fallen out of favor and into the boots of luck.

I've lived fully and sometimes not at all, and I've been guided by the examples and voices of people worldwide who took the time to authenticate my story. The coaches, the teachers, the employers, and the stewards of my experiences that I've been lucky to encounter through nearly five decades of life have all been a part of the tapestry that I lovingly call … my life. I thank you for seeing qualities in me that I might not have been ready to acknowledge or embrace.

Writing a book is not a solitary endeavor but a community event where one represents many. I am fortunate to have enduring friendships that have weathered time and distance. To my loving and patient wife, Christie, thank you for co-piloting a sometimes-foggy path with love, compassion, and an endless belief in me … and us. To my children, Heath and Whitley, thank you for your passion for life and thirst for competition, for doing what's right, and for putting up with me and my collection of dad jokes.

Christie, Heath, and Whitley have graced me with the grounding logic and love that allows this author, husband, and father to navigate the stories and time zones that fuel my imagination. I thank my loving trio for being the main characters in the story of my life. Marriage and parenthood have made my life complete.

I'm not a gambler in the purest sense, but I can recognize a good poker player who respects their opponent, the dealer, and the house. Countless professionals bet on "Berger" when the house might have chosen *red*. I am forever indebted to the storyteller community I proudly stake membership in—Wiley, The Jim Henson Company, Victor Yerrid, Halle Stanford, and core voices who know me now and knew me when— John Barnett, Landon Hutchison, Chuck May, Coach Hal Commerson, Richard Gerver, and Jamie YaYa Barry.

A final, closing acknowledgment to those who have graced my journey around the world, never prospecting for favor or suspicious of purpose: Thank you for unearthing the power of humanity through the trust of your stories. The value of your respective stories will forever yield strong emotions and vibrant memories.

—Rod

About the Author

Dr. Rod Berger is a keynote speaker, moderator, producer, and expert in strategic storytelling. He draws on more than 4,000 interviews conducted worldwide for *Forbes*, *Entrepreneur Magazine*, and *Fair Observer*, including a cover story about former Virgin executive Jason Felts for *Los Angeles Magazine*, as well as various podcasts. He has captured the narratives of investors, CEOs, renowned entrepreneurs, bestselling authors, scholars, and cultural icons such as NBA legends Magic Johnson and Charles Barkley, alongside United Nations officials and Van Halen's Sammy Hagar, while also exploring the behind-the-scenes world of Formula 1. Berger has met with the Crown Princess of Sweden, Pope Francis, United Nations officials, and NGO leaders, covering stories of water insecurity with WaterAid, the intergenerational refugee crisis faced by displaced Sudanese in Uganda, and the impacts of child marriage in Western Africa with the Le Korsa Foundation.

Berger served as a guest lecturer at Vanderbilt University's Owen Graduate School of Management for nearly two decades, focusing on the power of storytelling in business.

He has partnered with The Jim Henson Company to create a television show, *The Ultimate GOAT*, that combines his passion for distant lands and storytelling with culture, sports, and puppetry for family programming.

Berger conducts moderated keynote events that blend storytelling with live, on-stage narratives featuring cultural icons such as Opal Lee, the recipient of the Presidential Medal of Freedom, a nominee for the Nobel Peace Prize, and recognized as the "Grandmother" of Juneteenth. In 2023, Berger received the inaugural Pangea International Literacy Prize and delivered his TEDx Talk: *Story is Our Currency*. He lives in Nashville with his wife and two children.

Index

232 Index

Authenticity. *See also* Stories, selling of
  in communication, xiii–xiv
  connection through, 76, 170
  detachment from, 24
  from disparate elements, 135
  in interviews, 56
  and Law of Jante, 65, 72
  maintaining, 113
  in narrative, 154, 192
  from origin stories, 27–28
  in "our" perspective, 39
  power of, 99–116
  reflecting on, 214
  representation of, 5, 125
  as social equalizer, 59

B

Bad News Bears, 104
Barkley, Charles, 117–119
Beginnings (of stories), 16, 24, 84, 88, 97,
    112, 124, 141. *See also* Endings
    (of stories); Middles (of stories)
Belushi, Jim, 215
Best weapon benches, 90–91, 93–97.
    See also Dialogue benches
Board game stories, 137–154
  for children, 139–141
  concepts of, 153–154
  mentality of, 144
  permission in, 137, 153
  question method for, 143–145
  for teenagers, 141–144
Bombeck, Erma, 32–33
Braveheart, 108
Breitling, 159–162, 165–166, 170–172
Brite College, 183
Broenniman, Linda Ambrus, 205

C

Caine, Michael, 215
Candy Land (board game), 142, 144
Candyland Island Stories, 140, 142
Case stories, 188
Case studies, 151, 188
Chastain, Jessica, 189
ChatGPT, 179–180, 194

Choose Your Own Adventure books, 1
Christensen, Callie, 113
Civil Rights Movement, 92
Cohen, Peter, 166–167
Columbine High School, 141
Comfort, 46, 95, 135, 208–209, 211, 214
Comfort zones, 95–96
Coming-of-age stories, 20, 58, 214
Compassion, 53, 59, 83, 135, 190,
    201, 203, 209
Conflict, xi, 15–16, 66, 73, 75, 79, 123,
    160, 193. *See also* Negotiation
Context:
  importance of, 63–64, 162
  lack of, 57
  in origin stories, 27
  of personal stories, 178, 180
  providing, 145
  in story versions, 135
  of work, 110
Control:
  creative, 36
  lack of, 153
  of narrative, 25, 43, 128, 220
  and permission, 137
  releasing, 14–15
  of stories, 5, 21
  version, 118
Core values, 211
Cox, Courteney, 215
Cruise, Tom, 159

D

Damon, Matt, 20, 214
The Dark Crystal: Age of Resistance, ix–x
Data points, 108, 128, 151, 164, 172
Dayal, Manish, 188
Dead Man Walking, 144
Dead Poets Society, 106
Dehner, Stephane, 159
Denniz Pop Music Awards, 132
Department-specific terminology, 101
Detroit Pistons, 39–40, 119, 124, 126, 128
Dialogue, 88, 89–92, 96–97, 125, 187
Dialogue benches, 91, 96. *See also* Best
    weapon benches